Hands-on History

World History ACTIVITIES

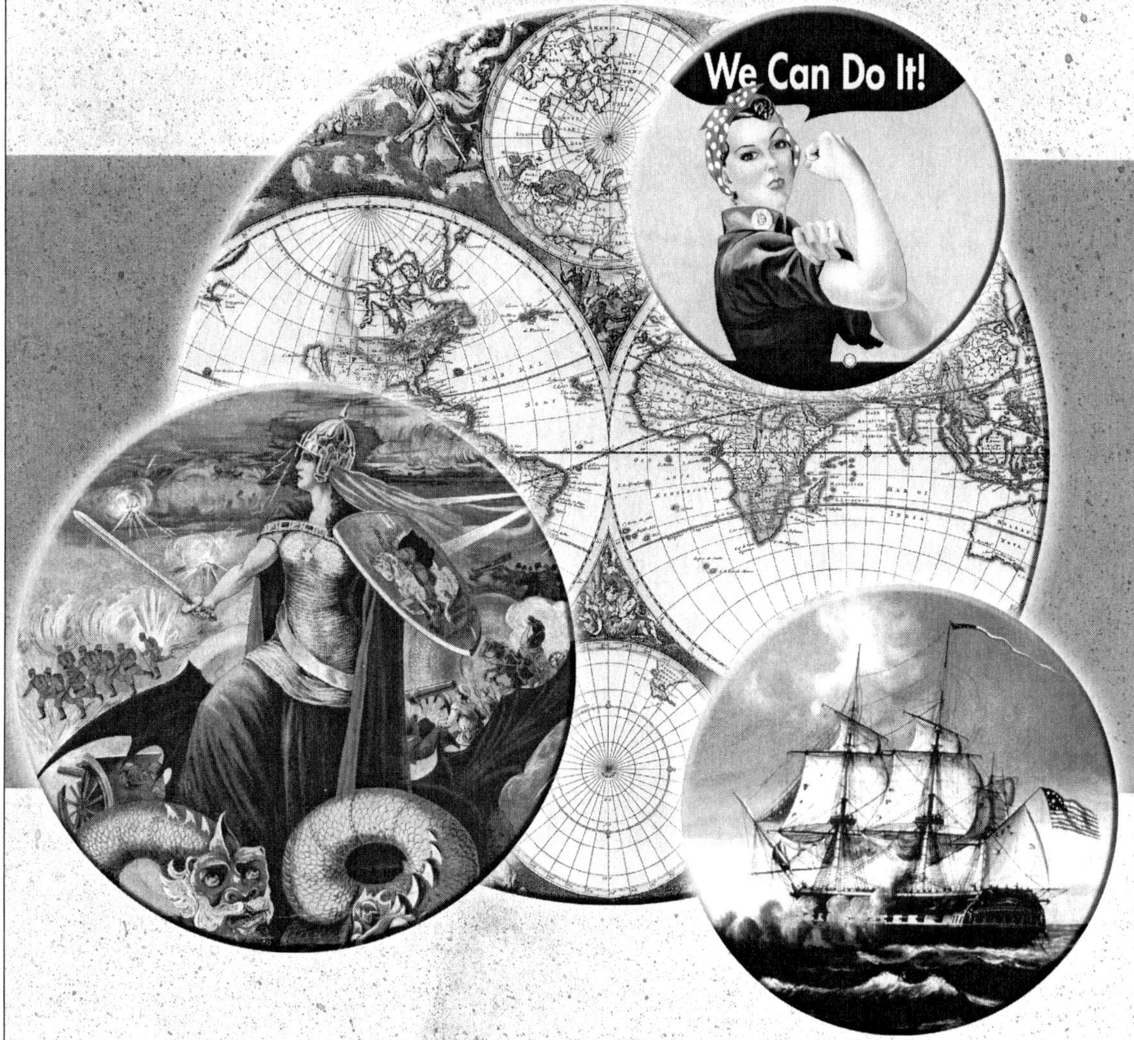

Authors

Garth Sundem, M.M. and Kristi A. Pikiewicz

Editor
Gillian Eve Makepeace

Editorial Project Manager
Emily R. Smith, M.A.Ed.

Editor-in-Chief
Sharon Coan, M.S.Ed.

Creative Director
Lee Aucoin

Production Manager
Peter Pulido

Editorial Manager
Gisela Lee, M.A.

Imaging
Phil Garcia

Illustration Manager/Designer
Timothy J. Bradley

Cover Designer
Lesley Palmer

Illustrators
Timothy J. Bradley
Ana Clark
Jaime Ortiz

Cover Art
Library of Congress
National Archives
Historical Documents Co.

Standards
National Council for the Social Studies, 1994
Compendium, Copyright 2004 McREL

Publisher
Corinne Burton, M.A.Ed.

Shell Education

5301 Oceanus Drive

Huntington Beach, CA 92649-1030

http://www.shelleducation.com

ISBN 978-1-4258-0382-7

©2006 Shell Educational Publishing, Inc.

Reprinted 2011

The classroom teacher may reproduce copies of materials in this book for classroom use only. The reproduction of any part for an entire school or school system is strictly prohibited. No part of this publication may be transmitted, stored, or recorded in any form without written permission from the publisher.

Table of Contents

Introduction 4

How to Use This Book 7

Overview of Activities 8

Correlation to Standards 10

The Byzantine and Muslim Empires **11–28**
   Lesson Plans 11
   Reproducibles 16

Civilizations of Africa **29–44**
   Lesson Plans 29
   Reproducibles 33

The Ancient Americas **45–77**
   Lesson Plans 45
   Reproducibles 50

Civilizations of Asia **78–110**
   Lesson Plans 78
   Reproducibles 84

Europe in the Middle Ages **111–140**
   Lesson Plans 111
   Reproducibles 118

Renaissance and Reformation **141–175**
   Lesson Plans 141
   Reproducibles 145

A Century of Turmoil: 1940–2001 . . . . **176–190**
   Lesson Plans 176
   Reproducibles 180

Scoring Guides 191

Introduction

It was hard to carry water from the bucket to the cup at my desk because my desk was far away, and that's why people wanted to live close to rivers. Also it was easier to work as a group than on your own because you could work together and get free time for art and inventing stuff, and that's why people formed societies.
—Sixth grade student in Bozeman, Montana

Research is now validating what teachers have known intuitively all along: hands-on learning increases retention and understanding.

Using both history and political science classes, the studies found that students who participated in the role-plays and collaborative exercises did better on subsequent standard evaluations than their traditionally instructed peers (McCarthy and Anderson 2000).

For example, students at a St. Louis middle school experimenting with hands-on learning methods have scored consistently higher on the Stanford Achievement Tests than those in other district schools (Harvey, Sirna, and Houlihan 1998). In other words, once a student has built the Great Wall of China out of salt dough, he or she will remember it forever. By linking learning with experience, we encourage students to remember information as part of this action.

In addition to increasing assessment scores, hands-on learning also increases student motivation. "Tactile learning activities generated positive evaluative attitudes in fifth-grade learners toward geography. These learners did better academically when their competence was measured by content tests" (Blahut and Nicely 1984). Students enjoy hands-on activities, and when students are motivated, they learn.

Though still new to the world of social studies, hands-on learning is not revolutionary in all teaching disciplines. Science teachers use an increasingly hands-on, experimental approach in their teaching.

Introduction (cont.)

Jean Piaget (1986) said the following about the need for a shift toward experimental learning in science education:

> A sufficient experimental training was believed to have been provided as long as the student had been introduced to the results of past experiments or had been allowed to watch demonstration experiments conducted by his teacher, as though it were possible to sit in rows on a wharf and learn to swim merely by watching grown-up swimmers in the water . . . the repetition of past experiments is still a long way from being the best way of exciting the spirit of invention . . .

It is in hopes of exciting the spirit of invention that we offer this book of social studies simulations. More precisely, these simulations and games are designed to excite the spirit of exploration, providing both the experiential basis of knowledge and also the spark of interest so needed to encourage further study. For example, while gaining an overview of a historic period through simulated daily life, students may also be competing as small groups to conquer neighboring groups. These games are cool in much the same way that a snowball fight is cool. By making your subject cool you immediately trick students into intellectual excitement and curiosity. For many teachers in the early and middle grades, sparking this excitement in later study is a goal unto itself.

Piaget also says that involvement is the key to intellectual development. Using these games, you will involve all students, each at their differentiated level of ability and each in their preferred method of learning. For example, in the course of an activity, you may split your class into small groups in which one student makes group decisions, another interacts with neighboring groups, other students are delegated to read background material and talk with their partners, while the remaining students work to complete hands-on design and construction projects. These classroom-tested simulations involve all five of your students' senses and allow students to choose the learning styles that are best for them.

Introduction *(cont.)*

The included simulations also offer many opportunities for small group interaction, encouraging a collaborative approach to learning, which is yet another strategy validated by research. "Total reading, language, mathematics, and battery scores indicated that students in the cooperative learning class scored higher than students in the traditional class" (Pratt and Moesner 1990).

Today is an exciting time in social studies education. More and more we are creating authentic experiences for our students, be they through simulations, active learning, or even evaluation of primary source materials. We are coming to respect that it is more powerful for students to walk through the rows of crosses at Arlington National Cemetery than it is to read the words of a historian. We see that exploring African American sheet music of the 1850s as archived by the American Memory Project at the Library of Congress creates a much more personal response to segregation in American history than simply discussing the issue as a class.

We hope this book helps you infuse your classroom with the light of discovery and learning, allows you to add richness to your students' experiences, and helps you show students that history is not dead. Social studies is alive, breathing, and evolving, and not only in a laboratory or research facility, but in your classroom. People today are part of the same culture and the web of history connects us all. Through experiencing and appreciating the goals, struggles, and decisions of past societies, students in your classroom will gain a deeper appreciation for the world-changing issues facing people today.

Blahut, John M., and Robert F. Nicely Jr. 1984. Tactile activities and learning attitudes. *Social Education* 48: 153–158.

Harvey, Barbara Z.; Richard T. Sirna; Margaret B. Houlihan. 1998. Learning by design: Hands-on learning. *American School Board Journal* 186: 22–25.

McCarthy, J. Patrick and Liam Anderson. 2000. Active learning techniques versus traditional teaching styles: Two experiments from history and political science. *Innovative Higher Education* 24: 279–294.

Piaget, Jean. 1986. Essay on necessity. *Human Development* 29: 301–314.

Pratt, Sherry J. and Cheryl Moesner. 1990. A comparative study of traditional and cooperative learning on student achievement. ERIC database #325258.

How to Use This Book

Welcome to *Hands-on History: World History Activities*. Included are activities for seven periods of history taught in the world history curriculum. While the goals of these activities are to create excitement and spark interest in further study, they are also firmly based in standards and include scoring guides and ideas for assessing student learning.

Through extensive classroom testing, we have found the best use of these activities is as an introduction to each world history unit. Many of the *Hands-on History* activities provide societal overviews in the course of role-playing activities. Students are motivated by winning a game, but they gain an informed impression of the civilization as a byproduct. Using these activities to prepare each unit, students come to look forward to the start of new periods of history and, having completed the game, will have the big picture in which to place further in-depth study. Alternately, as each unit stands alone, you can pick and choose which activities you would like to use and which you would rather leave for another year.

Be aware that some of these activities require significant preparation time. These are not everyday activities, but are the super-spectacular punctuation to which both you and your students can look forward. You will find that by organizing a general box of craft materials, you can significantly reduce the preparation time needed. You might also consider inviting motivated parents to join in the fun on activity days, adding another pair of able hands. All needed reproducibles and read-aloud directions are included within this book. So, you will find that once you organize the craft materials and form a clear picture of the game's directions in your head, the activity itself flows smoothly.

Also included are ideas for teacher-led class discussions, following the National Council for History Education (NCHE) History's Habits of Mind guidelines. We have frequently found that the post-activity discussions are reason enough to run the activity, as students extend the knowledge and experience gained during the activity to make connections to the world around them. Even young students have demonstrated the understanding necessary to discuss high-level questions, learned through their own hands-on exploration of the authentic problems faced by societies throughout history.

Feel free to personalize the activities, use only pieces of the activities, or expand and contract the class time as you see fit. Once you have run them a couple of times, you will undoubtedly find ways to emphasize elements that fit your specific curriculum goals and will find additional discussion topics that you wish to explore. Many activities can be presented in chunks allowing you to insert materials of your choice.

In today's classrooms, teachers have to deal with the seemingly opposing forces of a recognized need for discovery-based learning and an increased desire to teach the standards. These activities can help you successfully straddle the ideological fence. By encouraging teamwork, creativity, intelligent reflection, and decision making, the activities in this book will help you take a hands-on approach to teaching while inspiring your students to their own explorations of world history.

Overview of Activities

The Byzantine and Muslim Empires *(lesson on pages 11–15)*

Students will compete as Europe, the Far East, and the Middle East to create the most influential society, as shown by accumulating trade goods, wealth, and knowledge. Initially, the game gives Europe and the Far East a significant advantage, but each time these societies pass through the Byzantine and Muslim Empires of the Middle East, they pay with silver coins or with ideas. Eventually, due to their status as a trade hub, the Middle East becomes the dominant society of the time. Through cooperative group projects and interaction with neighboring societies, students will learn how trade influenced the spread of ideas and will gain an overview of the cultures and achievements of the Byzantine and Muslim Empires. This activity shows a snapshot of the three societies and allows students to preview the cultures and geography they will later be studying in depth. You will measure student learning through evaluation of small-group activities, discussion, and a short quiz. This activity includes cross-curricular connections in writing, art, and math.

Civilizations of Africa *(lesson on pages 29–32)*

After performing African folk tales as reader's theater plays and analyzing these plays for cultural significance, students will work as groups to match the performed folk tales to the cultures that created them. This activity will help students distinguish between the cultures of West, East, and South Africa while giving them an overview of Africa in the medieval period. Students will also learn how archaeologists study oral traditions and mythologies to learn about ancient cultures. This activity uses historically real folk tales, encourages content-area writing, and allows differentiation based on learning types. You will measure student learning through discussion and a short end-of-activity quiz.

The Ancient Americas *(lesson on pages 45–49)*

In this primarily individual activity, students will race to recreate a city of the Mayas, Aztecs, Incas, or Anasazi. Through completing a series of small tasks—during which students will learn about each society's culture—students will earn puzzle pieces that combine to create pictures of major cities built by the societies (Machu Picchu, Tenochtitlan, Tikal, or a pueblo). After earning all the puzzle pieces, students will interact with the map of their ancient cities in order to answer a series of map-based questions. Finally, all the students who worked on each civilization will discuss their answers and create a presentation, which they will give to the rest of the class. As tasks include hands-on projects as well as research and thinking skills, this activity allows students to use a variety of learning styles. You will evaluate student learning by assessing packets created during the activity, during discussion, and through a short end-of-activity quiz.

Civilizations of Asia *(lesson on pages 78–83)*

On three successive days, students will split into groups and complete tasks representing religion, government, and mythology. After each day, students will enter the information they find on a cardboard wheel, with the three types of tasks able to spin independently of each other. Once students have completed their tasks and have entered their information on the wheel, they will try to spin the dials on the wheel to match the correct information with India, China, and Japan, earning a classroom reward if they are correct. This activity promotes animated discussion and learning through discourse. You will measure student learning through discussion and an end-of-activity quiz.

Overview of Activities *(cont.)*

Europe in the Middle Ages *(lesson on pages 111–117)*

Students will work in small groups, each representing a feudal society, and will compete to be the first to build a castle. Groups will need to perform tasks that represent gathering the needed resources and expertise but will, at the same time, need to run their feudal cities. While the goal is to complete the castles, groups should not neglect the day-to-day workings of their societies, or they may (not) live to regret it. This game is fast-paced and fun, encouraging students to make quick decisions and act efficiently in order to beat other societies. As such, you will want to have a firm grasp of the rules before starting. You will measure student learning through discussion, observation, and a reflection quiz. This activity also includes content-area writing assignments and primary source materials.

Renaissance and Reformation *(lesson on pages 141–144)*

Working in small groups, students will role-play museum curators who are trying to match listed artifacts with the correct Renaissance country of origin. As information about each country's culture is provided in stages, students will revise their views of history based on changing information. After recreating works of art using the techniques of the chosen artworks, each group will present its country to the class and will place all the created artworks in its country's display in your classroom Renaissance Museum. Students will gain an overview of Renaissance history and culture and will also explore the difficulties in piecing together the past from incomplete information. As many of their initial artwork/country pairings will be wrong, students will learn the changing nature of history and the need for historical revision as new information comes to light. This activity uses primary source materials and incorporates art activities. Student learning will be measured through discussion, evaluation of activity sheets, and through a short quiz.

A Century of Turmoil: 1940–2001 *(lesson on pages 176–179)*

In this activity, students will explore online oral histories that describe some of the twentieth century's most difficult events, focusing on those that affected the United States. Specifically, students will compare the attitudes surrounding World War II, the Holocaust, and Pearl Harbor with the testimonies of September 11, 2001 survivors. Please be aware that this can be an emotionally difficult activity, and you will want to assign mature students to the 9/11 and Holocaust histories.

Depending on your technology resources, you can ask students to complete the activity individually, in small groups, or perform the research as a teacher-guided lesson by attaching a projector to one computer. Alternately (with older classes), you can have students complete the research portion of the activity as homework. In an optional extension, students may gather their own oral histories and present them to the class.

Correlation to Standards

Lesson Title	NCSS Process Standard	McREL Content Standard
The Byzantine and Muslim Empires	Examine, interpret, and analyze physical and cultural patterns and their interactions, such as land use, settlement patterns, cultural transmission of customs and ideas, and ecosystem changes. (III-h)	World History—Expanding Zones of Exchange and Encounter 300–1000 CE Standard 13—Understands the causes and consequences of the development of Islamic civilization between the 7th and 10th centuries.
Civilizations of Africa	Describe the role of specialization and exchange in the economic process. (VII-e)	World History—Expanding Zones of Exchange and Encounter 300–1000 CE Standard 16—Understands the development of agricultural societies and new states in tropical Africa and Oceania.
The Ancient Americas	Compare similarities and differences in the ways groups, societies, and cultures meet human needs and concerns. (I-a)	World History—Expanding Zones of Exchange and Encounter 300–1000 CE Standard 17—Understands the rise of centers of civilization in Mesoamerica and Andean South America in the 1st millennium CE.
Civilizations of Asia	Explain why individuals and groups respond differently to their physical and social environments and/or changes to them on the basis of shared assumptions, values, and beliefs. (I-d)	World History—Expanding Zones of Exchange and Encounter 300–1000 CE Standard 14—Understands major developments in East Asia and Southeast Asia in the era of the Tang dynasty from 600 to 900 CE.
Europe in the Middle Ages	Examine and describe the influence of culture on scientific and technological choices and advancement, such as in transportation, medicine, and warfare. (VIII-a)	World History—Intensified Hemispheric Interactions 1000–1500 CE Standard 20—Understands the redefinition of European society and culture from 1000 to 1300 CE.
Renaissance and Reformation	Demonstrate an understanding that different scholars may describe the same event or situation in different ways but must provide reasons or evidence for their views. (II-a)	World History—Global Expansion and Encounter 1450–1770 Standard 27—Understands how European society experienced political, economic, and cultural transformations in an age of global intercommunication between 1450 and 1750.
A Century of Turmoil: 1940–2001	Describe the ways nations and organizations respond to forces of unity and diversity affecting order and security. (VI-d)	World History—The 20th Century Since 1945 Standard 44—Understands the search for community, stability, and peace in an interdependent world.

The Byzantine and Muslim Empires Lesson Plans

The Byzantine and Muslim Empires

Overview

Students will compete as Europe, the Far East, and the Middle East to create the most influential society, as shown by accumulating trade goods, wealth, and knowledge. Initially, Europe and the Far East have a significant advantage, but each time these groups pass through the Byzantine and Muslim Empires of the Middle East, they pay with silver coins or with ideas. Eventually, due to its status as a trade hub, the Middle East becomes the dominant society of the time. Through cooperative group projects and interaction with neighboring societies students will learn how trade influenced the spread of ideas and will gain an overview of the cultures and achievements of the Byzantine and Muslim Empires. This activity shows a snapshot of the three societies and allows students to preview the cultures and geography they will later be studying in depth.

Camel chain in China
Source: Clipart.com

You will measure student learning through evaluation of small-group activities, discussion, and a short quiz. This activity includes cross-curricular connections in writing, art, and math.

Objectives

- Students will understand how geography affects the transmission of culture. (NCSS)
- Students will learn an overview of the dominant societies of the period A.D. 300–1000, focusing especially on the Byzantine and Muslim Empires.

Materials

- copies of reproducibles (pages 16–28) as described on page 12
- textbooks, encyclopedias, the Internet, or other research materials
- craft materials (cardboard, tape, glue, pens, construction paper, straws, etc.)
- 8 small bars of soap
- something to carve soap
- 3 oranges
- cloves (to poke into oranges)
- 5 plastic or Styrofoam cups
- dice

©Shell Educational Publishing   #9357 *Hands-on History: World History Activities*

The Byzantine and Muslim Empires (cont.)

Preparation

Total preparation time should be about 30 minutes.

1. Make an information packet for each group containing the following:
   - **Europe**—*Society Information: Europe* (page 18); *Rules of Trade* (page 17); *Trade Goods: Europe* (page 21); *Ideas: Europe* (page 24); 30 silver coins (page 16)
   - **The Middle East**—*Society Information: The Middle East* (page 19); *Rules of Trade* (page 17); *Trade Goods: The Middle East* (page 22); *Ideas: The Middle East* (page 25)
   - **The Far East**—*Society Information: The Far East* (page 20); *Rules of Trade* (page 17); *Trade Goods: The Far East* (page 23); *Ideas: The Far East* (page 26); 5 silver coins (page 16)
2. Organize a craft table with all the materials listed on page 11.
3. Photocopy and cut out an additional 40 silver coins (page 16). (Laminating silver coins would allow you to re-use them in future years.)
4. Make an overhead of the *Habits of Mind Discussion* (page 28).
5. Make a class set of the *Byzantine and Muslim Empires Quiz* (page 27).

Directions

1. After reading the *Read-Aloud Directions* (pages 13–14), place students in three groups representing Europe, the Far East, and the Middle East. Organize groups in the room geographically such that Europe is opposite the Far East, with the Middle East in the middle. Allow students time to look over their information packets.
2. Begin the activity. Groups will compete to fill the requirements of the *Society Information* sheets, with the first group to do so winning the game. First, they will create ideas and trade goods. Then, they will trade according to the rules on their *Rules of Trade* sheet.
3. Initially, it looks like Europe or the Far East has a major advantage over the Middle East, but as the game progresses, the Middle East should dominate. If other societies get close to winning (i.e., Europe), set them back with one of the *Barbarian Invasions* (page 15). Help students understand that these barbarian invasions are historically accurate.
4. Once the Middle East group fills the requirements of its *Society Information* sheet, close the activity with the *Habits of Mind Discussion* and the *Byzantine and Muslim Empires Quiz*.

Things to Consider

1. Penalize groups for any off-task behavior by taking silver coins or by asking them to "forget" one of their ideas.

The Byzantine and Muslim Empires (cont.)

Things to Consider (cont.)

2. While the game is heavily weighted in favor of the Middle East, it is still possible for another group to win. Guard against this with barbarian invasions and by ensuring the Middle East has its fair share of strong students. However, if another group wins, you can use this to discuss the role of chance in history.
3. One advantageous and historically accurate strategy that works well for the Middle Eastern society is to buy trade goods from China and resell them for a profit to the Europeans (and vice versa). You may want to hint at this strategy.
4. Students will need to be able to read and comprehend directions. With a younger class, you might want to spend additional time previewing the directions, especially the rules of trade.
5. War is generally a bad idea, though it is one that students are likely to try. Notice that the Middle East has Greek Fire, a weapon made from petroleum, and in the game using this allows them to add five to their defensive dice roll.

Read-Aloud Directions

Remember the ancient world, where everything was easy and societies generally had the common decency to exist only one at a time? First Mesopotamia, then Egypt, then Greece, then Rome. Sure there was a little overlap. (Remember that Antony and Cleopatra thing?) But, the societies of the ancient world generally behaved like a series of kings in one country, with one springing up to fill the space left by another.

But, eventually things got a little messed up. All of a sudden, everybody wanted a piece of history at the same time. Rome was still holding on, China and the Far East were everybody's favorite department store, and the Middle East was stuck in, well, the middle.

Today, you are going to split into these three societies and compete for influence in the changing world. You will be competing to gather wealth, trade goods, and ideas. The first group to fill the requirements for each of these three things will win the game. Trading is the most complex part of the game, so lets look at that now:

- Trade is generally good for both the buyer and the seller. It is also the only way to get the trade goods you need in order to win the game. (The goods you create yourself don't count as trade goods—they are only for selling.)
- You may only travel with one item of trade goods at a time, so you will have to make many trips.

The Byzantine and Muslim Empires (cont.)

Read-Aloud Directions (cont.)

- You can travel to buy or to sell, but cannot do both on the same trip.

- Any time you travel to or through a country you must give two of your idea markers and get one of their idea markers. You also need to pay the country you travel to, or through, one silver coin.

- When a country buys a trade good, the teacher will pay half the price. For example, if Europe bought silk in China, China would get three silver coins from Europe and three from the teacher.

- If you travel to buy, you will buy trade goods at the fixed price of six silver coins per item. If you travel to sell the trade goods you create, you can sell them for whatever price people will pay. (You will need to arrange your own price.)

- You may only trade if you have enough silver coins and ideas to pay the amount needed.

Example (traveling to buy): Europe goes to the Far East to buy silk. On the way there, Europe pays the Middle East two idea markers and one silver coin, and gets one idea marker. In China, Europe pays two idea markers and one silver coin, and gets one idea marker. Europe also buys silk for six silver coins (teacher pays half). On the way back, Europe again pays the Middle East two idea markers and a silver coin and gets one idea marker. Overall, Europe has spent three idea markers and six silver coins to gain the silk.

Example (traveling to sell): China brings one unit of silk to the Middle East to sell. China pays two idea markers and one silver coin and gets one idea marker. They arrange to sell their silk for ten silver coins (teacher pays half). Overall, China has spent an idea marker and has gained nine silver coins.

You can also attack other societies, but be careful—the cost of battle is high.

All the directions are included in your information packets, so don't worry if it sounds a bit complex right now. Also, don't be surprised when different societies start with different resources. We'll take time now to look over our information packets. Then, we will have a few minutes to ask questions. Remember to focus on trade goods, wealth, and ideas.

[Split students into groups, allow time for them to look over the information packets, answer any questions, and then begin the activity.]

The Byzantine and Muslim Empires   Lesson Plans

The Byzantine and Muslim Empires (cont.)

Barbarian Invasions

Announce one of these barbarian invasions if Europe or the Far East is close to winning the game. Use the Middle East invasion only to prolong the game.

Europe I

The Visigoths were a tribe of barbarians from Germany who invaded the Roman Empire from the north in A.D. 268. After many years of fighting and truces, the Visigoths under their strong leader, Alaric, sacked Rome in A.D. 410. Europe loses half their ideas and half their silver coins.

Europe II

Though the Vandals were from eastern Germany, they moved around until settling in northern Africa near the ancient city of Carthage. In A.D. 455 the Vandal King Geiseric led a force across the Mediterranean Sea and into Rome where they sacked the city for two weeks and carried off many valuable treasures. Europe loses half their ideas and half their silver coins.

The Far East

The Huns, called Xiong-Nu by the Chinese, were a nomadic tribe of warriors who had strongholds in both modern-day North Korea and in Hungary. Periodically the Huns, including those led by the feared Attila the Hun, would rampage through China using their superb horsemanship and weapons such as the Hun bow, which allowed the Huns to shoot long range from horseback, to crush their foes. During the Han dynasty, the Huns swept through China. China loses half their ideas and half their silver coins.

The Middle East

Crusade! The European world launches an attack against Muslims in what just about everybody (Christians, Muslims, Jews) considers their holy land. The First Crusade wasn't until A.D. 1096, but the Middle East still loses half their silver coins and half their ideas.

Answer Key

Byzantine and Muslim Empires Quiz (page 27)

1. C—Hinduism
2. B—perfume
3. A—silk
4. D—Aztec religion
5. B—A.D. 300–1000
6. Rome = Europe
   Byzantine Empire = The Middle East
   China = The Far East
   Muslim Empire = The Middle East
7. Answers will vary but should reference the interaction between cultures promoted by commerce.
8. Answers will vary but should include a description of trade from Europe and the Far East traveling through the Middle East.

The Byzantine and Muslim Empires   *Reproducibles*

Silver Coins

Rules of Trade

- Trade is generally good for both the buyer and the seller. It is also the only way to get the trade goods you need in order to win the game. (The goods you create yourself don't count as trade goods—they are only for selling.)

- You may only travel with one item of trade goods at a time, so you will have to make many trips.

- You can travel to buy or to sell, but cannot do both on the same trip.

- Any time you travel to or through a country, you must give two of your idea markers and get one of their idea markers. You also need to pay one silver coin to the country you travel to or through.

- When a country buys a trade good, the teacher will pay half the price. For example, if Europe bought silk in China, China would get three silver coins from Europe and three from the teacher.

- If you travel to buy, you will buy trade goods at the fixed price of six silver pieces per item. If you travel to sell the trade goods you create, you can sell them for whatever price people will pay. (You will need to arrange your own price.) Of course, if people come to you to buy, you will sell the goods you create for six silver pieces.

- You may only trade if you have enough silver coins and ideas to pay the needed amounts.

- You may only have one set of traders away at any given time.

The Byzantine and Muslim Empires *Reproducibles*

Society Information: Europe

Names: _____   Date: _____

You are the Roman Empire. After the rule of Julius Caesar and his nephew Octavian, you are no longer bound by laws but have a series of strong emperors with the power to do pretty much anything they want. Follow the rules below to create the most influential society in the changing world.

1. Your goal is to gather enough wealth, trade goods, and ideas to fill the bars at the bottom of this page. If you can fill them all, you win the game.

2. You gather wealth by selling the trade goods you create. You gather trade goods by buying them from other countries. (Your own goods do not count.) You gather ideas by creating them and receiving them when visited by another society.

3. All wealth (silver coins) looks the same, but you will create your own markers for trade goods and for ideas. Although these markers will look different, they are all worth the same value.

4. You will earn, gain, spend, and lose all the things you need (wealth, trade goods, ideas), so use a pencil to lightly fill in the bars at the bottom of this page.

5. Look at your *Trade Goods* sheet (page 21) for the rules of trade. Look at your *Ideas* sheet (page 24) for the rules of ideas.

6. Rules of war:
   - You can attack another society at any point.
   - It costs 20 silver coins to attack another country.
   - If you win, you will gain half the conquered country's wealth, ideas, and trade goods.
   - If you lose, you will have to pay the country you attacked half your wealth, trade goods, and ideas.
   - To decide the battle, you will roll dice against your opponent. Each society rolls two dice and adds to this score its number of ideas. (For example, if you rolled a 7 and had three idea markers, your total roll would be 10.) The society with the highest score wins the battle.

7. You will need to decide who in your group will be in charge of ideas, who will be in charge of trade goods, and who will be in charge of trading.

Wealth   ☐☐☐☐☐☐☐☐☐☐☐☐☐☐☐☐☐☐☐☐
Trade Goods ☐☐☐☐☐☐☐☐☐☐☐☐☐☐☐☐☐☐☐☐
Ideas   ☐☐☐☐☐☐☐☐☐☐☐☐☐☐☐☐☐☐☐☐

The Byzantine and Muslim Empires   *Reproducibles*

Society Information: The Middle East

Names: _____   Date: _____

You are the Byzantine and Muslim Empires of the Middle East. While you don't start as a wealthy region, you occupy a special place in relation to Europe and the Far East. Follow these rules to create the most influential society in the changing world.

1. Your goal is to gather enough wealth, trade goods, and ideas to fill the bars at the bottom of this page. If you can fill them all, you win the game.
2. You gather wealth by selling the trade goods you create. You gather trade goods by buying them from other countries. (Your own goods do not count.) You gather ideas by creating them and receiving them when visited by another society.
3. All wealth (silver coins) looks the same, but you will create your own markers for trade goods and for ideas. Though these markers will look different, they are all worth the same value.
4. You will earn, gain, spend, and lose all the things you need (wealth, trade goods, ideas), so use a pencil to fill in the bars at the bottom of this page.
5. Look at your *Trade Goods* sheet (page 22) for the rules of trade. Look at your *Ideas* sheet (page 25) for the rules of ideas.
6. Rules of war:
   - You can attack another society at any point.
   - It costs 20 silver coins to attack another country.
   - If you win, you will gain half the conquered country's wealth, ideas, and trade goods.
   - If you lose, you will have to pay the country you attacked half your wealth, trade goods, and ideas.
   - To decide the battle, you will roll dice against your opponent. Each society rolls two dice and adds to this score its number of ideas. (For example, if you rolled a 7 and had three idea markers, your total roll would be 10.) The society with the highest score wins the battle.
7. You will need to decide who in your group will be in charge of ideas, who will be in charge of trade goods, and who will be in charge of trading.
8. Secret: You have a special weapon called Greek Fire which you use to repel invaders. If you are attacked, add five to your dice score. You cannot use Greek Fire to attack.

Wealth   ☐☐☐☐☐☐☐☐☐☐☐☐☐☐☐☐☐☐☐☐☐☐☐☐☐☐☐☐☐☐
Trade Goods ☐☐☐☐☐☐☐☐☐☐☐☐☐☐☐☐☐☐☐☐☐☐☐☐☐☐☐☐☐☐
Ideas   ☐☐☐☐☐☐☐☐☐☐☐☐☐☐☐☐☐☐☐☐☐☐☐☐☐☐☐☐☐☐

©Shell Educational Publishing

The Byzantine and Muslim Empires   *Reproducibles*

Society Information: The Far East

Names: _____   Date: _____

You are the empire of China, famous for your exotic spices and beautiful silks. The wealth of your country depends on selling these goods to rich buyers in Europe and the Middle East. Follow the rules below to create the most influential society in the changing world.

1. Your goal is to gather enough wealth, trade goods, and ideas to fill the bars at the bottom of this page. If you can fill them all, you win the game.

2. You gather wealth by selling the trade goods you create. You gather trade goods by buying them from other countries. (Your own goods do not count.) You gather ideas by creating them and receiving them when visited by another society.

3. All wealth (silver coins) looks the same, but you will create your own markers for trade goods and for ideas. Though these markers will look different, they are all worth the same value.

4. You will earn, gain, spend, and lose all the things you need (wealth, trade goods, ideas), so use a pencil to lightly fill in the bars at the bottom of this page.

5. Look at your *Trade Goods* sheet (page 23) for the rules of trade. Look at your *Ideas* sheet (page 26) for the rules of ideas.

6. Rules of war:
   - You can attack another society at any point.
   - It costs 20 silver coins to attack another country.
   - If you win, you will gain half the conquered country's wealth, ideas, and trade goods.
   - If you lose, you will have to pay the country you attacked half your wealth, trade goods, and ideas.
   - To decide the battle, you will roll dice against your opponent. Each society rolls two dice and adds to this score its number of ideas. (For example, if you rolled a 7 and had three idea markers, your total roll would be 10.) The society with the highest score wins the battle.

7. You will need to decide who in your group will be in charge of ideas, who will be in charge of trade goods, and who will be in charge of trading.

Wealth   ☐☐☐☐☐☐☐☐☐☐☐☐☐☐☐☐☐☐☐☐

Trade Goods ☐☐☐☐☐☐☐☐☐☐☐☐☐☐☐☐☐☐☐☐

Ideas   ☐☐☐☐☐☐☐☐☐☐☐☐☐☐☐☐☐☐☐☐

The Byzantine and Muslim Empires   *Reproducibles*

Trade Goods: Europe

Names: _____   Date: _____

Directions: Complete the tasks below to earn goods that you can sell to other countries. If another society travels to you, you must sell them one trade good for six silver coins. If you travel elsewhere, you may sell your trade goods for whatever price you can get people to pay.

Bronze Work

Romans used a method called "lost-wax casting" to make their large bronze statues. In this technique, the sculptor first made a clay model and then covered this clay model with wax. Another layer of clay went over the wax. Artists then heated the "wax sandwich" and the wax melted out leaving a space into which they poured bronze. When the bronze hardened, they broke away the clay, leaving the metal statue.

Make a poster showing the lost-wax casting method. Your poster needs to be colorful and needs to include an illustration of each step in the casting process. You may make two posters to sell to other societies.

Wool Textiles

Roman shepherds produced fine wool and artisans wove this wool into patterned clothing, which the Romans traded throughout the empire.

Get two sheets of paper of different colors. Cut the paper lengthwise into strips about one-inch wide. Now, find a way to weave these paper strips together as shown to the right. Staple or tape the edges so your paper does not unravel. You may make four paper weaves to sell to other societies. (Remember to use two full sheets of paper for each paper weave.)

Olive Oil

Olives were cultivated in what is present-day Italy as early as 600 B.C. They were so important that legend holds that the city of Athens chose Athena's gift of an olive tree over Poseidon's offer of good trade on the seas. That's why the city is named Athens.

Use craft materials to create a *mola olearia*, as shown to the right. The *mola olearia* was pushed in a circle, and the huge stone wheels would crush olives in the vat, creating olive oil. You may create three *mola olearias* to sell to other societies.

The Byzantine and Muslim Empires *Reproducibles*

Trade Goods: The Middle East

Names: _____ Date: _____

Directions: Complete the tasks below to earn goods that you can sell to other countries. If another society travels to you, you must sell them one trade good for six silver coins. If you travel elsewhere, you may sell your trade goods for whatever price you can get people to pay.

Perfumes

Perfumes were an important export and those made from frankincense and myrrh were especially prized by the Romans. By A.D. 1, the Romans used 2,800 tons of frankincense and 550 tons of myrrh every year. The Middle East also traded rose water with China, where it was thought to aid digestion and liver function. Many perfumes were transported in jars made from clamshells.

On a piece of colored paper, write what you think perfume would be used for in this time period. Your description needs to be at least four sentences long. Be creative—you might describe a scene as if it were a story! Then, fold this paper into a fan so that it looks like the bottom of a giant clamshell. You may create three perfume clams to sell to other societies. (Each description needs to be different.)

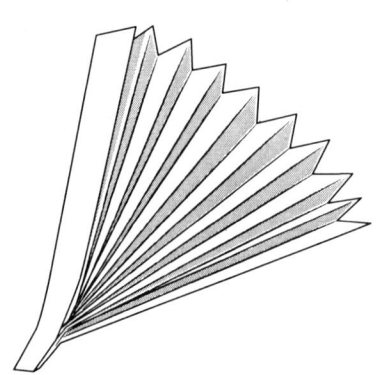

Paper Mill

Paper was invented in the Far East, but the great paper mills of Baghdad in the Middle East were the first to mass-produce it. First, linen rags were soaked in water until they started to fall apart. Then the rags were boiled and cleaned. Next, the rags were beaten until they turned into pulp. Once Muslim papermakers had pulp, they pressed it into sheets of paper, which were then dried on huge racks.

Make a poster showing the stages of papermaking. Your poster needs to be colorful and needs to include an illustration of each stage in the papermaking process. You may create three papermaking posters to sell to other societies.

Obsidian, Lapis Lazuli, and Turquoise

The Middle East was (and still is) rich in precious stones. From mines in Persia, these stones were traded to Europe and to the Far East. The Egyptians made expeditions to Persia to mine turquoise. Later, turquoise was carved with scenes from the Islamic Koran (sacred text).

Carefully carve four small bars of soap with scenes from around your school. You can sell each of these four pieces of jewelry to other societies.

The Byzantine and Muslim Empires — *Reproducibles*

Trade Goods: The Far East

Names: _____ Date: _____

Directions: Complete the tasks below to earn goods that you can sell to other countries. If another society travels to you, you must sell them one trade good for six silver coins. If you travel elsewhere, you may sell your trade goods for whatever price you can get people to pay.

Silk

Silk was the most important export for China and the Far East. As you might know, silk comes from worms. Silkworms spin cocoons out of long lengths of silk. In China, peasants gathered these cocoons and unraveled them along wheels until they had the long threads. From one cocoon, peasants could unwind 1,000 meters of silk! Once they had many long threads, they wove them into fabric. Silk threads are so thin that you need 100 cocoons to make one necktie or 650 cocoons to make a woman's blouse.

Cut a piece of construction paper into four parts. Using one of these squares, write and illustrate the process of silk making. You can make eight of these descriptions to sell to other societies.

Spices

Spices were very important in the medieval world. Most of the time there wasn't much choice in foods—vegetables were only available for a short period of the year, and without refrigeration, meat spoiled quickly. People needed spices to make food taste better. Most spices came from southern China and even from India, where nutmeg and cloves grew.

Poke cloves into oranges until the oranges are mostly covered. You may create three of these spiced oranges to sell to other societies.

Incense

Burning incense didn't just smell nice—Romans burned incense in their temples as part of religious ceremonies. This practice became part of the Christian and Islamic religions.

Cut a piece of construction paper into four parts. On each of these pieces of paper, draw a picture of people performing a religious ritual. Now, shave soap until you have a small pile. Glue these soap shavings to your pictures to create a good-smelling religious ritual. You may create eight of these decorated rituals to sell to other cultures.

The Byzantine and Muslim Empires　　　　　　　　　　　　　　　　Reproducibles

Ideas: Europe

Names: _____　　Date: _____

Directions: Complete these tasks and then create idea markers to show your learning. You may earn up to ten idea markers for each of the tasks below. Remember, you need idea markers to travel and to trade. You also need ideas to win the game.

Philosophy and Ancient Learning

Romans kept alive the learning of ancient Greece, which included advances in architecture, thought, mathematics, and poetry. Certain poems, called *Epinicians*, told the stories of great victories at the ancient Olympic Games.

Write a poem about a great event of our time. This event can be sports, or it might be something else. Your poem doesn't need to rhyme, but it needs to be at least four lines.

For every poem you write, you may create one idea marker. Cut out a small cardboard circle, write an *E* on one side, and then write *Epinician* on the other side.

Christianity

Although Christianity started in the Middle East, the Roman Emperor Constantine made Christianity the official religion of the Roman Empire in A.D. 312. He also gave land and money to the Christian Church and did not make the church pay taxes.

Use your textbook, encyclopedias, the Internet, or other classroom resources to research Christianity. Keep a list of the facts you find.

For every two facts you write, you may create one idea marker. Cut out a small cardboard circle, write a large *E* on one side, and then draw a cross on the other side.

Republic

From 510 B.C. until A.D. 44, Rome was a republic, which means that it was governed by laws. Even though there were powerful people in the republic, these people still needed to follow the written laws. The United States is also a republic.

Make up your own laws for Europe. Also write punishments for breaking these laws. Be creative!

For every two laws/punishments you write, you may also create one idea marker. Cut out a small cardboard circle, write a large *E* on one side, and then write *Republic* on the other side.

The Byzantine and Muslim Empires   *Reproducibles*

Ideas: The Middle East

Names: _____ Date: _____

Directions: Complete these tasks and then create idea markers to show your learning. You may earn up to ten idea markers for each of the tasks below. Remember, you need idea markers to travel and to trade. You also need ideas to win the game.

Five Pillars of Islam

The religion of Islam was founded by the prophet Muhammad in A.D. 610. Like the teachings of Judaism and Christianity, those of Islam are contained in a holy book, called the Koran. The Koran tells of the five pillars of Islam: faith, prayer, sharing, fasting, and *hajj*. *Hajj* is a sacred journey to Mecca.

Use craft supplies to create a model of a pillar. Your pillar needs to stand on its own and needs to be at least six inches tall. Write the five pillars of Islam on your pillar.

For every pillar you create, you may make one idea marker. Cut out a small cardboard circle, write a large *M* on one side, and then write *Pillar* on the other side.

Algebra

While the Arabic numerals that we use today are originally from India, the Muslim Empire of the Middle East was the first society to use them to solve complex problems. In fact, you have the Muslim Empire to thank for the math classes you have in school. Before this time, societies used Roman numerals or systems of slash marks.

Write math word problems. For example, *In two years, Matt will be twice as old as Kara is now. Kara is 12 years old. How old is Matt?*

For every problem you write and solve, you may create one idea marker. Cut out a small cardboard circle, write a large *M* on one side, and then write *Numbers* on the other side.

Poetry

Some people are good at everything, like Leonardo da Vinci and Benjamin Franklin. Another person who was good at everything was Omar Khayyam. He lived in the golden age of Islam and was a great astronomer, mathematician, and poet. Omar Khayyam wrote the following words:

> *When I was a child, I sometimes went to a teacher.*
>
> *And sometimes I taught myself, but eventually I learned*
>
> *The limits to all knowledge: we come into this world upon*
>
> *the waters, we leave it on the wind.*

Write poetry in the style of Omar Khayyam. Each poem needs to be at least four lines.

For each poem you write, you may make two idea markers. Cut out a small cardboard circle, write a large *M* on one side, and then write *Khayyam* on the other side.

The Byzantine and Muslim Empires   *Reproducibles*

Ideas: Far East

Names: _____ Date: _____

Directions: Complete these tasks and then create idea markers to show your learning. You may earn up to ten idea markers for each of the tasks below. Remember, you need idea markers to travel and to trade. You also need ideas to win the game.

Compass

The Chinese were the first to use the magnetic compass, which helped them navigate by sea. (They were also the first to use the boat rudder.) Because of their seafaring skills, the Chinese were able to trade with the spice-rich islands of Southeast Asia and with faraway societies such as India.

Use your textbook or other classroom resources to draw small maps of Asia and the surrounding areas. You need to include China, Egypt, the Middle East (Persia), Europe, and India.

For each map you draw, you may make one idea marker. Cut out a small cardboard circle, write a large *F* on one side, and then write *Maps* on the other side.

Wheelbarrow

By the fifth century A.D., every culture in the Mediterranean region knew about the wheel. But, China was the only one that used the wheelbarrow, which allowed one worker to carry the load of many. General Chuko Liang is credited with the invention of the wheelbarrow, around the year A.D. 200. He used the wheelbarrow to transport supplies and injured soldiers.

Cut a cup in half to use as the bed of your wheelbarrow and then use craft supplies to add a wheel and handles. Be creative!

For every wheelbarrow you create, you can make two idea markers. Cut out a small cardboard circle, write a large *F* on one side, and then draw a picture of a wheelbarrow on the other side.

Buddhism, Taoism, and Confucianism

The Chinese of this period had both religions and philosophies. The religions of Taoism and Buddhism talked about what happens after you die and used elements of magic and belief. The philosophy of Confucianism told people how to live their daily life according to the principles of order. People could be both Taoist and Confucian.

Use your textbook, encyclopedias, the Internet, or other classroom resources to research these three ways of thought. Keep a list of the facts you discover.

For every two facts that you write, you may create one idea marker. Cut a circle out of cardboard, write a large *F* on one side, and then write *Three Ways of Thought* on the other side.

The Byzantine and Muslim Empires   *Reproducibles*

Byzantine and Muslim Empires Quiz

Name: _____ Date: _____

Directions: Circle the best answer to each question below.

1. Which was **NOT** a system of belief common to China?
    - A. Buddhism
    - B. Taoism
    - C. Hinduism
    - D. Confucianism

2. Which is an export of the Middle East?
    - A. olive oil
    - B. perfume
    - C. silk
    - D. bronze statues

3. What was the most important export of the Far East?
    - A. silk
    - B. wool textiles
    - C. precious stones
    - D. perfume

4. Which idea did **NOT** travel along the Silk Road?
    - A. Christianity
    - B. Islam
    - C. technology
    - D. Aztec religion

5. Which time period best describes the Byzantine and Muslim Empires?
    - A. 750 B.C.–A.D. 1
    - B. A.D. 300–1000
    - C. A.D. 1–300
    - D. A.D. 1000–1500

6. Draw a line to connect each society with its geographical region. You will have more than one line going to some geographical regions.

Society	Geographical Region
Rome	The Middle East
Byzantine Empire	The Far East
China	Europe
Muslim Empire	

7. How did the Silk Road help the spread of ideas?

_____

8. How did their geographical position help the Byzantine and Muslim Empires?

_____

Habits of Mind Discussion

- How did trade influence the spread of ideas?

- How did trade influence wealth and power?

- How did military technology influence the balance of power?

- What was each society's major strength?

- Which of the three societies in this activity do you think the United States is most like? Why?

Civilizations of Africa   Lesson Plans

Civilizations of Africa

Overview

After performing African folk tales as reader's theater plays and analyzing these plays for cultural significance, students will work as groups to match the performed folk tales to the appropriate cultures. This activity will help students distinguish among the cultures of West, East, and South Africa while giving them an overview of Africa in the medieval period. Students will also learn how archaeologists study oral traditions to learn about ancient cultures.

This activity uses historically real folk tales, encourages content-area writing, and allows differentiation based on learning types. You will measure student learning through discussion and a short end-of-activity quiz.

African landscape
Source: Corel

Objectives

- Students will understand how specialized production of goods and supply-and-demand trade routes influenced the development of various African societies. (NCSS)
- Students will gain a cultural overview of West, East, and South Africa in the medieval period.

Materials

- copies of reproducibles (pages 33–44) as described on page 30
- craft supplies of your choice for use in creating props

Civilizations of Africa (cont.)

Preparation

Total preparation time should be about 15 minutes.

1. Make copies of each of the scripts (pages 35–42). If you like, laminate them for future use.
2. Make three copies of *Who's Doing What?* (page 33) and *What Do You Know?* (page 34).
3. Make an overhead of the *Habits of Mind Discussion* (page 44)
4. Make a class set of the *Civilizations of Africa Quiz* (page 43).

Directions

1. After reading the *Read-Aloud Directions* (page 31), place students in three groups and assign them areas of the room in which to rehearse.
2. Distribute scripts to each group and ask each group to complete a *Who's Doing What?* sheet.
3. If time permits, allow students the entire period to rehearse their plays, and encourage students with leading roles to practice their lines at home. You can also ask students who are creating props to gather supplies and finish their work at home.
4. Perform the three reader's theater plays.
5. Distribute a *What Do You Know?* sheet to each group and allow time for completion.
6. Read aloud the *Real Society Information* (page 32), and allow time for students to discuss, as a group, which society they think created their folk tale.
7. Reveal which society created which folk tale (see page 32) and discuss the clues that led students to their guesses.
8. Close with the *Habits of Mind Discussion* (page 44) and if you choose, give students the *Civilizations of Africa Quiz*.

Optional Introduction: Read aloud one of the many African folk tale picture books, such as *Anansi Goes Fishing* by Eric Kimmel.

Optional Extension: Before performing the plays, have students research medieval African culture and have them bring in food and music, creating an African festival on the day you perform the plays. If you like, invite parents or another class to be an audience.

Things to Consider

1. Groups will be working independently to rehearse and stage their reader's theater plays. Make sure groups elect responsible directors or choose the directors for them.
2. This activity has the potential to be completed in a period or to be stretched into multiple days. Before starting the activity, choose how you will use classroom time.

Civilizations of Africa (cont.)

Things to Consider (cont.)

3. Allowing students to choose their own roles and assigning others to create props can lead to students feeling left out of the performance. Be sure to emphasize the importance of the set designers and gather interesting materials for use in creating props.
4. In a younger class, you might have set designers create hang-around-the-neck nametags for each character so the roles are clear.
5. Much of the information tested in the short quiz is presented on the *Real Society Information* sheet rather than in the plays themselves. If giving the quiz, plan to spend more time discussing this sheet.

Read-Aloud Directions

Every culture has its own folk tales. In the United States, you might have heard about Paul Bunyan and Babe the Blue Ox, or you might have heard about Bigfoot, or maybe you've heard a famous ghost story. These are all examples of folk tales, and by hearing these folk tales, you can learn about the culture of the United States. For example, by hearing about Paul Bunyan and Babe the Blue Ox, you would learn about what life was like in a logging camp.

The same was true in medieval Africa. Each culture had its own stories, and by studying these stories we can learn what life was like at the time. In fact, much of the information that archaeologists know about medieval Africa comes from studying folk tales. In Africa, storytellers called griots passed folk tales from generation to generation using oral tradition, which means they told the stories aloud instead of writing them down. In modern Africa, there are still griots who keep their culture's oral tradition alive.

We are going to explore the folk tales of Africa. We will split into three groups and each group will perform a reader's theater of a folk tale that is from East, West, or South Africa. After performing the folk tales, you will learn a little about each society, and then you will have to guess where your folk tale is from.

The first step is to choose who is doing what. Some people will be actors and some will be set designers who will be responsible for making all the cool props you need for your performance. Each group will also have a director who is responsible for running your rehearsal. Listen to your director—he or she is in charge. Once you have filled out and shown me a *Who's Doing What?* sheet, you may start practicing your play. *[Split students into three groups, distribute a Who's Doing What? sheet to each group, and begin the activity.]*

Civilizations of Africa (cont.)

Real Society Information

East Africa

By A.D. 1200, there were 30 city-states that dotted the eastern coast of Africa. These city-states traded by sea with India and China to the east and by land with the civilizations of the Mediterranean to the northwest. They also had contact with Muslim traders from the Middle East. They eventually developed a language called Swahili that used the basics of Bantu but added many Muslim words. These city-states along the African coast were quite advanced—the city of Kilwa had beautiful fruit orchards that were watered by a system of streams and waterfalls.

West Africa

The civilizations of West Africa were also built on trade, but they were very different from their seafaring neighbors to the east. West African trade consisted of camel caravans through the great Sahara Desert. The Mediterranean civilizations wanted gold from West Africa. And, the West Africans needed salt from the north to stay alive. Cities such as Tombouctou, Walata, and Kumbi Saleh sprang up along these trade routes, mostly on the sites of desert oases.

South Africa

About 2,000 years ago, the Bantu people migrated east and south from West Africa. Eventually, the Bantu developed civilizations in South Africa and renamed themselves. Today, tribes such as the Maasai and the Zulu trace their ancestry to Bantu roots. The Zulu are famous for their stories in which animal actions explain the natural world.

Answer Key

Civilizations of Africa Quiz (page 43)

1. C—West Africa
2. C—East Africa
3. A—South Africa
4. A—trade
5. B—A.D. 750–1200
6. Answers will vary, but should include a discussion of the items, people, animals, and climate mentioned in folk tales.

Folk tale Matching Answers

Folk tale 1: Man's and Woman's New Skins—Zimbabwe, South Africa

Folk tale 2: The Game Board—Ethiopia, East Africa

Folk tale 3: The Chief's Clever Wife—Ghana, West Africa

Civilizations of Africa *Reproducibles*

Who's Doing What?

Directions: Before you rehearse your play, decide who is playing each part and who will be creating props. Look through your play, and write down each part. Then, assign people to these roles. Also, write down which props (things) you need for your play, and then assign people to make these props.

Part or Prop	Student

Civilizations of Africa *Reproducibles*

What Do You Know?

Names: _____   Date: _____

Directions: Fill out this sheet to discover which society created your folk tale.

Folk tale title: _____

1. Which animals are mentioned in the folk tale?
   _____
   _____

2. What is the climate of the area in your folk tale (hot, cold, wet, dry)?
   _____

3. Do the characters in your folk tale meet anybody interesting?
   _____
   _____

4. List three things you know about your society's culture from reading this folk tale.
   _____
   _____
   _____

5. List at least two other clues you found in your folk tale.
   _____
   _____
   _____

Folk Tale 1: Man's and Woman's New Skins

Narrator: After the Creator had finished making the world, he sat back in the heavens, very pleased with his work. He was especially proud of man and woman.

Creator: I am very pleased with my work. I especially like man and woman.

Narrator: See? Anyway, the Creator watched as the people he made fell and scraped their knees, whacked their thumbs with hammers, and dropped rocks on their toes.

Creator: I wish these people were a little less clumsy. Oh well, it looks like it's time for new bodies!

Narrator: So the Creator called Chameleon.

Creator: Come here Chameleon! The people of Earth are too clumsy and have messed up the nice bodies I made for them. I want you to take this package to man and woman. Tell them I sent you and do not delay!

Narrator: The Creator handed Chameleon a small package, and Chameleon set off to deliver it to man and woman. In these days, Chameleon was very fast and he made it down to Earth in no time at all.

Chameleon: Whew! I am sooooo fast. It looks like I have time to stop here at the river for a quick drink of water.

Narrator: But Chameleon wasn't the only animal drinking at the river that day.

Snake: Hello, cousin. What brings you down to Earth today?

Chameleon: Hello, Snake. I have a package to deliver for Creator. It's something for man and woman.

Snake: I don't like the people at all.

Narrator: Snake was sick of the people stepping on him and his family, and he was jealous of the attention that man and woman got from the Creator. When Snake heard that Chameleon was carrying a gift for the people, Snake started to scheme.

Snake: Hmmmmmm, how can I keep the people from getting that gift?

Narrator: And then Snake had an idea—an awful idea. The Snake got a wonderful, awful idea!

Civilizations of Africa   *Reproducibles*

Folk Tale 1: Man's and Woman's New Skins *(cont.)*

Snake: I know just what to do!

Narrator: The Snake laughed in his throat.

Snake: Oh dear cousin, Chameleon! My family has missed you. You never come over for dinner. Do you think that you are too good for us?

Narrator: Chameleon was very sensitive and wanted Snake to like him.

Chameleon: No, cousin, of course not! I would be honored to visit your family sometime!

Snake: Well, why not right now? My wife has a meal all prepared for me. Why don't you join us?

Narrator: Now, Chameleon knew he had to deliver the package to man and woman as quickly as possible, but he didn't want to offend his cousin.

Chameleon: Dear, cousin Snake, I really need to deliver this package to man and woman. What if I come over some other time?

Snake: Just as I thought—you think you are too good to dine with my family! That's okay (sob!), run along and take care of your business with man and woman, which I'm sure is more important than the feelings of my family.

Chameleon: Well, I guess the sun is still high in the sky. You know what, Snake? I would be honored to have a meal with you now. I will deliver the package to man and woman after we eat.

Narrator: So, Snake and Chameleon went back to Snake's house. Snake's wife had prepared a huge meal of *bobotie*, *koeksisters*, and Cape Malay pickled fish.

Snake's Wife: Try the *bobotie*. It's my favorite. And while you're here, why not have a nice glass of *utshwala*?

Chameleon: Don't mind if I do.

Folk Tale 1: Man and Woman's New Skins *(cont.)*

Narrator: Chameleon ate and drank and drank and ate, and his eyelids got heavier and heavier. Soon Chameleon fell fast asleep and Snake let out a little chuckle.

Snake: *Chuckle.*

Snake's Wife: What's so funny, my husband? It is a compliment that our guest has fallen asleep. It is the way of nature for creatures to sleep through the hot afternoon.

Snake: Look here.

Narrator: Snake hissed out another chuckle and gently lifted the package out from under Chameleon's arm.

Snake's Wife: What is it?

Snake: A gift to us from Creator!

Narrator: And Snake greedily tore open the wrapping paper.

Snake: Look! New skins, so that when our old ones wear out, we can just slip into new ones!

Narrator: Snake laughed so loud that Chameleon woke up. When Chameleon saw Snake with the skins, he knew immediately what had happened.

Chameleon: No Snake! Those skins are not for you. They are a gift from Creator to the people. Give them back!

Snake: No cousin, these are my skins now!

Narrator: Snake slithered away with the new skins and Chameleon felt awful. Chameleon slunk away into the forest where he climbed into the tree branches to hide from Creator, moving slowly so that he wouldn't be seen. And this is how people were cheated out of their new skins and why Snake can shed his old skin and grow a new one. But while Snake got the skins, they didn't solve his problems with people—they still stood on him, and most times when people saw Snake, they gave him what they thought he deserved: a good kick!

Civilizations of Africa *Reproducibles*

Folk Tale 2: The Game Board

Narrator: A man in the town of Nebri loved his son very much, so he carved him a beautiful game board, called a gebeta board, from the wood of an olive tree. The boy loved the gift and took it with him everywhere. Whenever he had time, he would stop and play games on his gebeta board.

Father: Nothing like a fine gebeta board to keep a young boy out of trouble!

Narrator: One morning when the boy was in the valley tending his cattle, he came upon a group of traveling Somalis with their camels. They were carrying salt to trade for gold. The Somalis were gathered around a small and dying fire that they had built in the shelter of the dry riverbed.

Somalis: Dear boy, where can we find wood for our fire in this country of yours?

Boy: I have wood right here.

Narrator: The boy gave the Somalis his fine gebeta board, which they burned in their fire. The boy began to cry.

Somalis: Don't cry! Here is a new knife in place of your gebeta board.

Boy: Thank you!

Narrator: It was a beautiful knife, decorated with scenes from Egypt. The boy went away with his cattle. Soon, he came across a man who was digging in the sand of the dry riverbed.

Man: Ah the ground is so hard! How will I ever dig deep enough to find water so that my goats can drink?

Boy: If you like, you can dig with my knife.

Man: Thank you!

Narrator: The man took the knife and used it to dig through the hard ground. Just as he found water, the blade of the knife snapped in two. The boy began to cry.

Boy: Oh what has become of my knife!

Man: Don't cry! Here is a spear in place of your knife.

Narrator: The man gave the boy a fine spear decorated with copper. The boy took the spear and left with his cattle. Soon he came across a party of hunters who were stalking a lion.

Hunters: Boy, lend us your spear so that we can kill this lion we have been trailing.

Boy: Well, I haven't had much luck today with loaning out my stuff, but . . . okay. Here's the spear.

Narrator: The hunters followed the lion and killed it with the spear, but in the hunt, the shaft of the spear shattered into a thousand pieces.

Folk Tale 2: The Game Board *(cont.)*

Boy: Oh what has become of my spear!

Hunters: Don't cry! Here is a horse in place of your spear.

Boy: A horse, wow!

Narrator: The boy took the horse and left with his cattle. On the way back toward the village, the boy passed a group of workers who were repairing the road. One of the workers accidentally kicked a rock from high up a steep hillside, and this rock started a landslide. The landslide was so loud that the horse became frightened and ran away.

Boy: Oh no! What has become of my horse?

Workers: Don't cry! We're sorry we made your horse run away. Here is an iron ax in place of your horse.

Boy: Well that's not such a good trade, but I guess it's better than nothing.

Narrator: So the boy took the ax and left with his cattle. As the boy continued toward the village, he came across a woodcutter chopping an olive tree with a small, rusty ax.

Woodcutter: Dear boy, lend me your ax so that I might chop down this tree.

Boy: Here we go again.

Narrator: The boy lent his ax to the woodcutter, who chopped down the tree. But, on the final swing, the ax broke into a thousand pieces.

Boy: Oh no! My ax!

Woodcutter: I'm sorry about your ax. Here—you can have a limb of this tree.

Boy: Oh . . . a tree branch . . . how nice.

Narrator: The boy took the branch and continued on his way with the cattle. Soon he came across an old woman who was making corn tortillas over a fire.

Old Woman: Ooh, firewood! How kind of you, young boy!

Boy: Well, actually I had planned to . . .

Narrator: But the old woman took the branch and put it into her fire.

Old Woman: Don't worry. Here is a fine gebeta board in place of your stick.

Boy: This looks familiar.

Narrator: The boy took the gebeta board and left with his cattle. Finally, he reached his village.

Father: Ah! Nothing like a fine gebeta board to keep a small boy out of trouble!

Civilizations of Africa   *Reproducibles*

Folk Tale 3: The Chief's Clever Wife

Narrator: Once there was a wise chief in the kingdom of Aksum. He had become wealthy through trading with India and China across the seas. Whenever his people had problems, they would bring them to the chief, who sat amid the streams and waterfalls of his fruit orchards. The chief was famous for solving his people's difficulties.

Old Man: Help me! My neighbor has stolen from me!

Chief: Slow down, old man. What, exactly, is the problem?

Old Man: My neighbor stole fruit from my orchard and I am too poor to replace it!

Neighbor: I don't know what he's talking about! I have fruit, but none of it belongs to this man.

Narrator: This was the type of problem the wise chief enjoyed the most.

Chief: I have a test for the two of you. I want to know what is the fastest thing in the world. The first person to bring me the answer will own the fruit.

Narrator: The two men were puzzled and went home to think. The old man repeated the question to his daughter Ziah, who was as beautiful as she was wise.

Ziah: Never fear father, I have the answer to the chief's riddle.

Narrator: She whispered the answer in her father's ear, and he returned to the Chief.

Chief: You have an answer for me already, old man?

Old Man: Yes, it wasn't that hard after all.

Chief: So, what is the fastest thing in the world?

Old Man: Time is the fastest thing in the world. We never have enough of it, and there is never enough time to do all the things that we want.

Chief: I am very impressed! Of course the fruit will be yours. But who helped you answer this riddle? Where did you get these words?

Old Man: They are my own words. Nobody helped me!

Chief: If you are lying, I will punish you!

Civilizations of Africa   *Reproducibles*

Folk Tale 3: The Chief's Clever Wife *(cont.)*

Old Man: Okay, okay. My daughter Ziah helped me. She is the one who answered your riddle. She is as beautiful as she is wise.

Chief: Hmmmm. I would like to meet this woman.

Narrator: So the old man returned home and brought Ziah before the chief.

Chief: Wow. I see you are as beautiful as you are wise. Will you marry me?

Ziah: Of course I will marry you, wise chief.

Chief: Great! I have only one rule: never involve yourself with the problems that people bring to me.

Narrator: The chief was afraid that Ziah was so wise that her solutions might be even better than his and that she would make him look bad by solving people's problems.

Chief: If you break this one rule, I will send you from my house.

Narrator: Ziah smiled and the chief had himself a new wife. For a while things went smoothly, with the chief continuing to solve people's problems. Most of the time, Ziah agreed with her husband's decisions. One day, two boys came to the chief. Both claimed ownership of a sheep.

Chief: I will give you two boys one of my famous puzzles. Here is an egg for each of you. Whoever can hatch their egg by tomorrow will own the sheep.

Narrator: There was one boy who obviously owned the sheep, and he was so upset that Ziah couldn't just sit by and watch him lose.

Ziah: I can't just sit by and watch you lose! Here is the answer to the chief's riddle.

Narrator: Ziah whispered the answer into the boy's ear and the boy ran off to find the chief.

Boy: Chief! I have the answer to your riddle!

Chief: Okay, let's hear it.

Boy: Here is some rice. Plant this rice today so that in the morning you will have rice to feed the chicken that hatches from the egg.

Folk Tale 3: The Chief's Clever Wife (cont.)

Chief: Ha! It is impossible to grow rice in a day!

Boy: Just as it is impossible to grow rice in a day, so too is it impossible to hatch an egg in a day!

Chief: Those words are too wise for a child your age! Who told you the answer to my riddle?

Boy: Nobody told me the answer. They are my own words!

Chief: If you are not speaking the truth, I will punish you!

Boy: Okay, okay. Ziah told me the answer!

Chief: Ziah! You have broken the only rule I set for you. Now go back to your father's home!

Ziah: Dear husband, before I go may I fix you one last meal? After you eat, I will take what is mine and return to my father's home.

Chief: Hmmm, I am a bit hungry. Okay. You may fix me one last meal and then take whatever you want and go.

Narrator: Ziah prepared the chief's favorite meal, which she flavored with spices from India and served with cups of palm wine. Soon the chief fell sound asleep. With her family's help, Ziah carried the chief back to her father's house. The next morning, the chief's voice boomed through the small house.

Chief: Where am I? What happened? What am I doing here?

Ziah: You said I could take whatever I wanted from your house. I wanted you so I took you.

Chief: You certainly are as wise as you are beautiful. Come, return with me to our home. Only a fool would send away such a wise and beautiful woman.

Ziah: And you, my chief, are no fool.

Civilizations of Africa   Reproducibles

Civilizations of Africa Quiz

Name: _____   Date: _____

Directions: Circle the best answer to each question below.

1. Which society would be most likely to trade salt for gold using a caravan of camels?

    A. South Africa   C. West Africa
    B. East Africa   D. China

2. Which society would be most likely to trade with India, China, and South Asia?

    A. South Africa
    B. West Africa
    C. East Africa
    D. Spain

3. In which society lived descendents of the Bantu people called the Maasai and Zulu?

    A. South Africa   C. West Africa
    B. East Africa   D. the Middle East

4. How did most African societies earn their wealth?

    A. trade
    B. agriculture
    C. fishing
    D. art and folk tales

5. What time period best describes the height of medieval African society?

    A. 500 B.C.–A.D. 1   C. A.D. 1–750
    B. A.D. 750–1200   D. A.D. 1200–1700

6. Describe how and what archaeologists learn about a culture by studying folk tales.

    _____
    _____
    _____
    _____

Habits of Mind Discussion

- What did we learn about African culture from these folk tales?

- Obviously, everything in folk tales is not true—how do you think archaeologists find truth in these tales?

- What are some folk tales you know, and what do they say about the cultures that created them?

- Would you have liked to live in East, West, or South Africa? Why?

- Do you think that oral tradition is a good way of transmitting history and culture? Why? Do you think oral tradition does a better job of transmitting history or culture?

- How do we pass down our traditions today?

The Ancient Americas

Overview

In this primarily individual activity, students will race to recreate a city of the Mayas, Aztecs, Incas, or Anasazi. Through completing a series of small tasks—during which students will learn about each society's culture—students will earn puzzle pieces that combine to create pictures of major cities or dwellings built by their societies (Machu Picchu, Tenochtitlan, Tikal, or a pueblo). After earning all the puzzle pieces, students will interact with the maps of their ancient cities in order to answer a series of map-based questions. Finally, all the students who worked on each civilization will discuss their answers and create presentations, which they will give to the rest of the class.

As tasks include hands-on projects as well as research and thinking skills, this activity allows students to use a variety of learning styles. You will evaluate student learning by assessing packets created during the activity, during discussion, and through a short end-of-activity quiz.

Aztec goddess, Coatlicue
Source: Clipart.com

Objectives

- Students will compare the similarities and differences in the ways groups, societies, and cultures meet human concerns. (NCSS)
- Students will learn about the major achievements of the Mayas, Aztecs, Incas, and Anasazi while gaining a cultural overview of each.

Materials

- copies of reproducibles (pages 50–77) as described on page 46
- textbooks, encyclopedias, the Internet, or other research materials
- cardboard
- flour, at least 5 lbs (2.25 kg)
- glue
- pens
- salt dough or clay (optional)
- salt, at least 26 oz (728 g)
- 4 bars of soap
- tape

The Ancient Americas (cont.)

Preparation

Total preparation time should be about 15 minutes.

1. Make a packet for each student that includes the sheets for their culture (for example, in a class of 24, you would need six Inca packets, six Aztec packets, etc.). Students will not be writing in these packets, so they are reusable with other classes (consider laminating). Include the following materials:
   - **Mayan packet:** Mayan activity sheets (pages 54–59), any non-Mayan puzzle sheet
   - **Anasazi packet:** Anasazi activity sheets (pages 60–64), any non-Anasazi puzzle sheet
   - **Incan packet:** Incan activity sheets (pages 65–69), any non-Incan puzzle sheet
   - **Aztec packet:** Aztec activity sheets (pages 70–74), any non-Aztec puzzle sheet
2. Make a class set of the *Map Evaluation* sheet (page 75) and the *Ancient Americas Quiz* (page 76).
3. Organize a table of craft materials.
4. Make an overhead of the *Habits of Mind Discussion* (page 77).

Directions

1. After reading the *Read-Aloud Directions* (pages 47–48), distribute packets to students such that the four civilizations are evenly distributed.
2. Have students cut out the puzzle pieces from the "other" societies included in their packets. They should paper-clip the pieces together and hand them in. (This saves you the preparation time needed to cut the puzzle pieces yourself.)
3. Allow students ample time to work independently on the tasks described in their packet. They may complete these tasks in any order and should choose tasks based on the materials and space available. Some of these tasks require students to work with partners.
4. For every task students complete, give them one puzzle piece. Notice that puzzle pieces are numbered to ease organization—for example, if students complete their third Incan task, they would get the Machu Picchu piece numbered *3*.
5. Once students earn all five puzzle pieces, give them *Map Evaluation* sheets. They will study their puzzles/maps to complete the sheet. (This is the only sheet on which students should write.)
6. The first student to complete the *Map Evaluation* sheet "wins," though you should continue the game until the majority of students are finished. (Those who finish may help their peers.)
7. Have groups of students who worked on the same civilizations meet in different sections of the room to discuss their civilizations and to create presentations to give to the class. Ask students to be sure to describe each task they had to complete as well as the answers to the *Map Evaluation* sheet.
8. Have each civilization present its information to the class and then discuss the group's findings.
9. Close with the *Habits of Mind Discussion* and give students the *Ancient Americas Quiz*.

The Ancient Americas *(cont.)*

Things to Consider

1. Students will be working independently for the majority of this activity. You may need to remind students that their *Map Evaluation* and *Ancient Americas Quiz* sheets will be graded.
2. As students will be working on different tasks at different times, it will deplete your time if you need to answer questions about every task. Either spend time previewing each task before beginning the activity, or let students know that figuring out the written directions is part of the activity's challenge.
3. If a good number of your students don't finish in the designated time, allow students to finish their packets as homework (especially if they have reached the *Map Evaluation* sheet, which depends less on access to craft materials).
4. You may need to support students who have difficulty reading by pairing them with able partners.

Read-Aloud Directions

How many ancient or medieval civilizations can you name that were around the Mediterranean Sea? What facts do you know about these places?

Okay, now how many ancient civilizations can you name that were in the Americas? What facts do you know about these people? Do you think it's strange to know more about faraway lands like Egypt than you know about the people of your own continent?

For the next few days we will be exploring the cultures of the Inca, Aztecs, Mayas, and Anasazi, looking especially at the most important city of each. The Aztecs built Tenochtitlan (tay-nohch-teet-LAWN), the Mayas built Tikal, the Incas built Machu Picchu (MAH-choo PEEK-choo), and the Anasazi built many cliff dwellings and pueblos in the desert Southwest. You will work individually to finish a packet of materials that has to do with one of these cultures. However, some tasks ask that you work with a partner or in a group of three—follow the directions listed on each sheet. Answer any questions on your own paper instead of writing in the packet! At the end of this activity, you will be turning in your projects and questions for a grade, so please keep all your work neat and organized. And, don't forget to put your name on everything.

For each packet task you finish, you will earn a puzzle piece. You do not have to complete the tasks in order. Look around to see what supplies are not being used to decide what to work on. Once you have collected all five puzzle pieces, put them together correctly, and show them to me. At that time, I will give you another task

The Ancient Americas (cont.)

Read-Aloud Directions (cont.)

to complete. The first person to complete their packet, the puzzle, and the final task will win the game. Once you've all finished, you will create presentations with the people who worked on the same civilizations as you. You will present your tasks, city, and any information you discover to the rest of the class.

Now, I will pass out the packets. Once you get your society packet, you may begin. Again, follow the directions on each sheet to earn puzzle pieces.

[Distribute packets and begin the game.]

Answer Key

Reference this page for answers to the various activity sheets and to the quiz.

Mayas: Calendar (pages 54–55)
1. Students should label the glyphs starting at the top, and then continuing counterclockwise.
2. 8
3. 260
4. 365

Mayas: Milpa (page 56)
1. Answers will vary but should reference the fact that there was little natural farmland in the rain forest.
2. Answers will vary but should include: need to constantly move; allowed only low population density; harmful to environment; and other answers as well.
3. Mayas would have had more time to create lasting culture (arts, science, etc.).

Mayas: Religion (page 57)
Working in teams, students should create colorful posters depicting Mayan religion.

Mayas: Pottery (page 58)
Students will mix and use salt dough to create replicas of Mayan pottery.

Mayas: Mathematics (page 59)
1. 40
2. 184
3. 218
4. 30
5. 377
6. 306

Anasazi: Basket Makers (page 60)
Students should weave together strips of paper to create "cloth."

Anasazi: Kokopelli (page 61)
Students should write and illustrate a short Kokopelli myth.

Anasazi: History (page 62)
1. Southwest (or geographical equivalent)
2. Earthenware pottery, above ground dwellings, irrigation, bow and arrow, etc.
3. A.D. 700
4. Cliff dwellings and pueblos (architecture)
5. To gather heat from the sun
6. Students should list two sites of Anasazi ruins.

The Ancient Americas (cont.)

Answer Key (cont.)

Anasazi: Pithouse and Kiva (page 63)
Working in pairs, students should create either a pithouse or a kiva. (If you cannot tell which, students will need to continue working.)

Anasazi: Pueblo (page 64)
Students will work in pairs to create a labeled poster of a pueblo including a basic written description.

Inca: Roads and Runners (page 65)
Students should create a poster showing the Inca Empire and South America and should include a short description of the Inca system of roads and message runners.

Inca: Stone Carving (page 66)
Students should carve soap into at least five blocks and use them to build a "stone" wall, which they will mount on cardboard.

Inca: End of the Empire (page 67)
1. 1532
2. They tricked the Inca ruler, Atahualpa.
3. Machu Picchu
4. Smallpox
5. Cuzco
6. Answers will vary.

Inca: Terraced Farming (page 68)
Students will work in pairs to create a model of terraced farming, including a short written description.

Inca: Quipus (page 69)
Students should work with partners to create a quipu and should be able to explain what the strings and knots in their quipu represent.

Aztec: Goddess Myth (page 70)
Working in pairs or in groups of three, students will create an illustrated book showing the Aztec creation myth.

Aztec: Floating Gardens (page 71)
Students work in pairs to create a poster of an Aztec chinampa (floating garden), including a short written description.

Aztec: Founding Myth (page 72)
1. Mexico
2. Mexico City
3. Answers will vary but should include reference to the difficulties of building a city in a swamp.

Aztec: Codex (page 73)
Students create a fold-out codex (like a book or scroll) with cardboard covers.

Aztec: Writing (page 74)
In their codex, students create at least 20 "Aztec" symbols with English translations and then use these symbols to write a sentence.

Ancient Americas Quiz (page 76)
1. C
2. D
3. A
4. C
5. B
6. D
7. Answers will vary, but students should describe one of the four cities in appropriate detail.

The Ancient Americas *Reproducibles*

Mayan Puzzle: Tikal

Source: Kim Copeland

The Ancient Americas   *Reproducibles*

Anasazi Puzzle: Pueblo Bonito

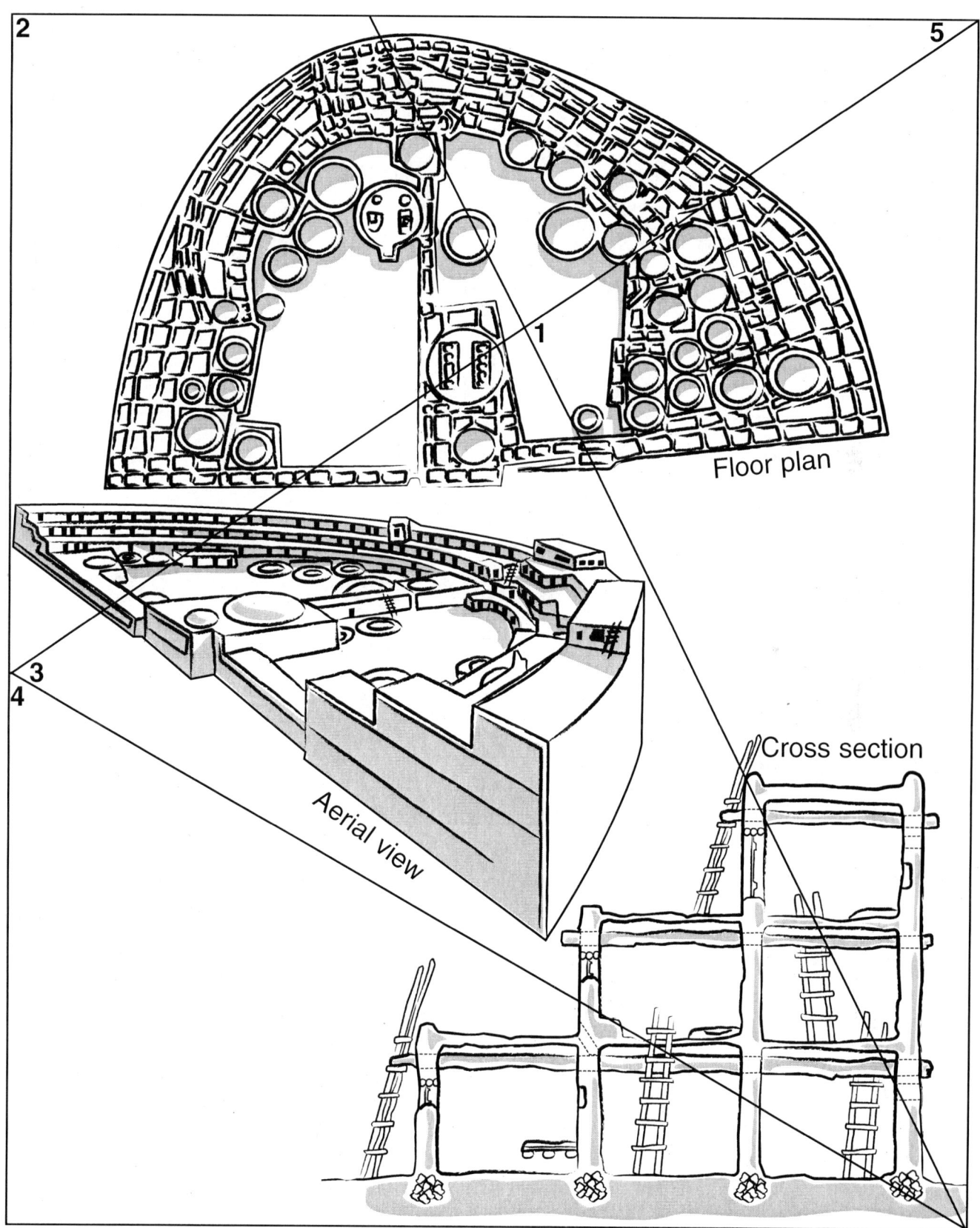

The Ancient Americas *Reproducibles*

Aztec Puzzle: Tenochtitlan

The Ancient Americas   *Reproducibles*

Inca Puzzle: Machu Picchu

The Ancient Americas   **Reproducibles**

Mayas: Calendar

Name: _____   Date: _____

Directions: Answer all four questions. When you are finished, show your work to your teacher to earn a puzzle piece. This is the hardest sheet in the entire activity! Make sure you read the questions slowly and do your best!

The Mayas used different calendars to keep track of different kinds of time. The main calendars were the *tzolkin* (zol-KIN) and the *haab*. The *tzolkin* measured the religious year, and the *haab* measured the solar year. The *haab was* like our calendar. A *tzolkin* calendar is shown on the next page.

1. The Mayas had 20 different names for days (like our seven named days), which you can see in the chart below. Look at the *tzolkin* and the glyph of the water lily at the top, labeled *Imix*. This is day number one and the days continue anticlockwise. Using the chart, label the other 19 glyphs on the *tzolkin*.

Imix	water lily	**Chuwen**	monkey
Ik	wind	**Eb**	tooth
Ak'bal	night	**Ben**	reed
K'an	corn	**Ix**	jaguar
Chikchan	snake	**Men**	eagle
Kimi	death head	**Kib**	soul
Manik	hand	**Kaban**	Earth
Lamat	venus	**Etz'nab**	flint
Muluk	water	**Kawak**	storm cloud
Ok	dog	**Ahaw**	lord

2. The Mayas also had 13 numbers for their days. The Mayas counted the day names and numbers in order, using two discs as shown on the next page. If you rolled the inside disc like a gear, what number would *Lamat* be?

3. When the Mayas rolled the small disc all the way around, they started over, so the first *Imix* would be *Imix*-1. If there are 20 named days and 13 numbered days, how many total days were there in the *tzolkin* calendar? (How many days until you would come to *Imix*-1, again?)

4. In the *haab* calendar, there were 18 months of 20 days each, and five unlucky days that were not named. How many total days were there in the *haab* calendar?

The Ancient Americas   *Reproducibles*

Mayas: Calendar (cont.)

Name: _____   Date: _____

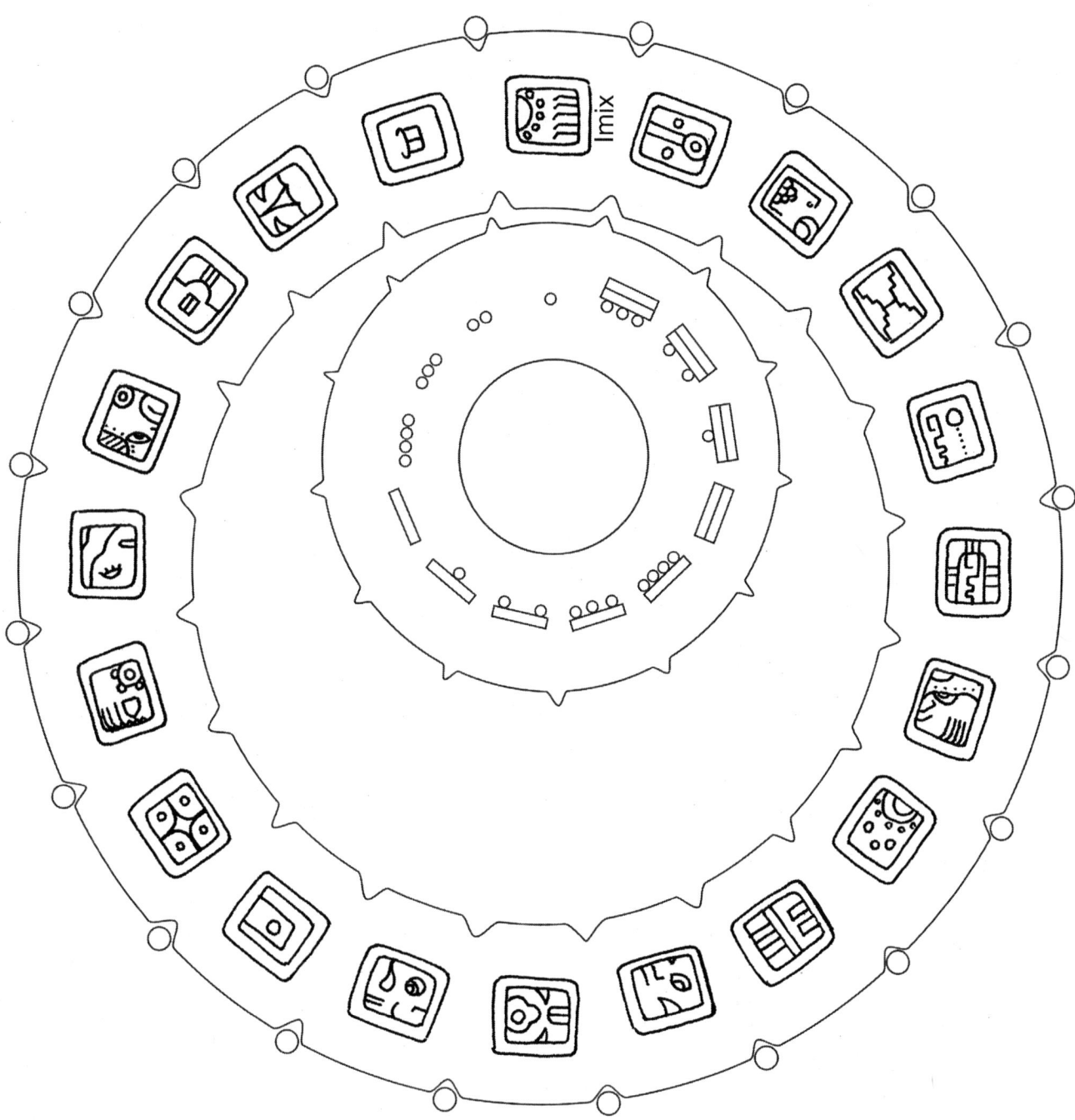

The Ancient Americas   *Reproducibles*

Mayas: Milpa

Name: _____   Date: _____

Directions: Answer the three questions. When you are finished, show your answers to your teacher to earn a puzzle piece.

Because of all the plants and animals in the rain forest, you might think the soil would be full of nutrients and it would be easy to grow things. Actually, there are so many trees and plants that almost all of the nutrients have already been sucked up, so it's hard to grow things in the rain forest.

The Mayas used a farming technique they called *milpa*. Today, this is called slash-and-burn farming. In *milpa*, the Mayas cut down a section of the rain forest and burned it so that the ash would provide fertilizer for their crops. After two to four years, all the fertilizer would be used up.

1. Why did the Mayas need to use *milpa* farming?

   _____

   _____

2. List three disadvantages to *milpa* farming.

   _____

   _____

   _____

   _____

3. To make a living, the Mayas needed to spend 220 days per year farming. How do you think Mayan society would have been different if it had been easier to grow food?

   _____

   _____

   _____

   _____

   _____

The Ancient Americas   *Reproducibles*

Mayas: Religion

Name: _____   Date: _____

Directions: Read the text below, then follow the directions. When you are finished, show your poster to your teacher to earn a puzzle piece.

The Mayan priests lived in temple cities such as Tikal. There peasants brought them food and the priests were able to spend all day studying the heavens. Unfortunately, priests were also an important part of sacrifices. Mayas believed the earth needed human blood in order to make crops grow. It was the priests' job to cut themselves and spill their own blood on the earth. The more important the priest, the more blood he was required to give.

It wasn't until later years that the Mayas actually adopted the practice of human sacrifice. The Mayas would drown volunteers who believed that by being sacrificed, they would go to heaven.

The Mayan sacred book, called the *Popol Vuh*, tells that the first man and woman were created from cornmeal.

Directions: Work individually or with a partner to make a poster showing some aspects of Mayan religion. Your poster needs to be colorful and needs to include as much written information as possible from the description above. Look at the pictures below to get ideas.

Source: Corel

©Shell Educational Publishing

The Ancient Americas *Reproducibles*

Mayas: Pottery

Name: _____ Date: _____

Directions: Read the text below, then follow the directions. When you are finished, show your art to your teacher to earn a puzzle piece.

Pottery made from clay was important to the Mayan people for art and for everyday use. First, the Maya collected clay from riverbeds. Then, they mixed this clay with temper (pieces of ash or sand) and formed the clay into pottery by piecing together slabs or by making long coils of clay and winding them. The Maya didn't use the pottery wheel. Once the pottery had dried to the consistency of leather, the Maya painted it with yellow, purple, red, and orange dyes, called *slips*.

Mayan artists were educated and rich, and most of their art shows kings and queens. The example on the left shows a king accepting the gift of a necklace from a merchant. The pottery on the right was most likely made by someone in the farming class. It would have used for storing grains.

 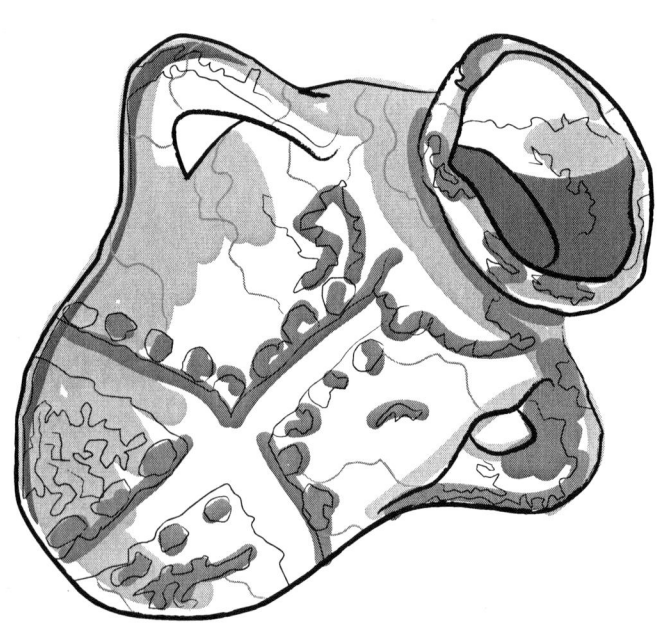

Directions: Work with a partner or in a group of three. Choose one of these items to recreate. Instead of clay and temper, you will use flour and salt. Mix four parts flour with one part salt (for example, four cups of flour and one cup of salt), and add just enough water to make it mushy. If someone else has completed this task, this step might already be done for you and you may use their extra dough. Use this dough to make your pottery. Leave it to dry overnight, and then decorate it with pens or paints.

The Ancient Americas   Reproducibles

Mayas: Mathematics

Name: _____   Date: _____

Directions: Read the text below, then follow the directions. When you are finished, show your answers to your teacher to earn a puzzle piece.

The Mayas had a very advanced system of mathematics, which was way ahead of mathematics in Europe. Instead of counting by tens, as we do, the Mayas used a system of numbers based on 20. Here is how the Mayas counted from zero to 19.

0	1	2	3	4
5	6	7	8	9
10	11	12	13	14
15	16	17	18	19

When the Mayas reached 20, they added another row. Here is how a Maya would write the number 24. The one dot is for 20 and the four dots are for 4.

Below is how Mayas would write the number 133. There are six 20s and thirteen ones.

Directions: Write the correct modern number below each of these Mayan numbers.

1.	2.	3.	4.	5.	6.

The Ancient Americas — *Reproducibles*

Anasazi: Basket Makers

Name: _____ Date: _____

Directions: Read the text below, then follow the directions. When you are finished, show your paper weaving to your teacher to earn a puzzle piece.

The early Anasazi were called Basket Makers. The Basket Makers, whose culture lasted until A.D. 550, wove bags, sandals, and baskets out of willow and yucca fibers. There were two ways to make baskets—the coil and the plait techniques.

Coiled baskets looked like spirals, which started small at the bottom of the pot and coiled around and around until the whole basket was made of one long strand, like the picture to the right.

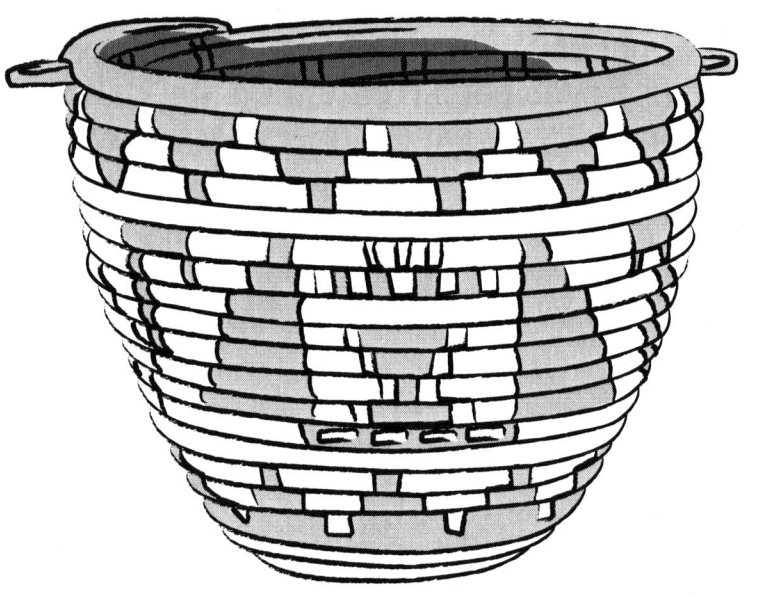

Plaited baskets were made by weaving in what's called a twill pattern (shown below). The Anasazi used plaited baskets for storage and for sifting flour. They even smeared the baskets with sticky pitch and used them to carry water. The picture below is called an "over-three, under-three" twill because each strip goes over three others and then under three others.

Directions: Cut one-inch (2.5 cm) wide strips of paper and figure out how to weave them as in the drawing to the left to create a section of plaited twill. Tape the edges of your twill so that it doesn't unravel. Once you have successfully completed seven rows of twill (as shown to the left), show the twill to your teacher.

The Ancient Americas   *Reproducibles*

Anasazi: Kokopelli

Name: _____   Date: _____

Directions: Read the text below, then follow the directions. When you are finished, show your myth to your teacher to earn a puzzle piece.

Kokopelli was the Anasazi trickster god. He was like Pan in Greek myths or Anansi the spider or the Jackal in African myths. In addition to being a trickster, the Anasazi believed that Kokopelli was a healer, magician, teacher, trader, god of the harvest, and god of fertility. Look at the picture of Kokopelli below.

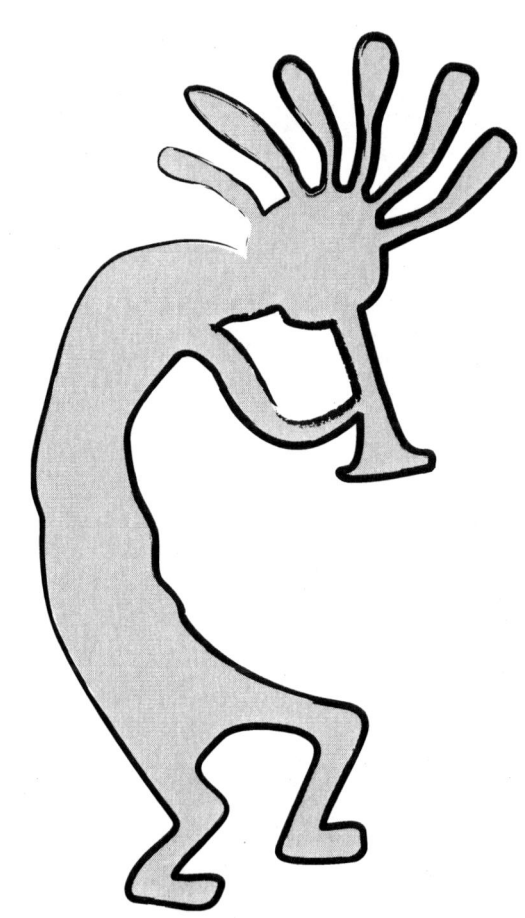

Usually Kokopelli is shown with a humpback and a flute. Sometimes he carries a bag of corn on his back. His ceremonial headdress always has an even number of feathers. Kokopelli has been around for more than 2,000 years and is still worshipped by many American Indian groups of the Southwest.

Directions: Write a short Kokopelli myth. First, decide what Kokopelli will be in your story—a trickster, healer, magician, teacher, trader, or god. Next, decide what he will do. Now, write your story and illustrate it using colored pencils or pens.

The Ancient Americas   *Reproducibles*

Anasazi: History

Name: _____   Date: _____

Directions: Read the text below, then follow the directions. When you are finished, show your answers to your teacher to earn a puzzle piece.

The Anasazi lived in the Southwest desert in an area known today as Four Corners. This is where Utah, Arizona, New Mexico, and Colorado touch. It was a dry area filled with canyons and mountains. It was hot in the summer and could get very cold in the winter. The Anasazi farmed corn, beans, and squash. They hunted animals including the pronghorn antelope and deer.

The ancestors of the Anasazi were called Basket Makers, after their beautiful baskets woven from plant materials. We would consider the Basket Makers fairly primitive. They lived in caves, wore furs, and hadn't yet discovered the bow and arrow.

The Anasazi developed from the Basket Makers in about A.D. 700. The main developments of the Anasazi were irrigation, terraced farming, pottery, and more permanent architecture. The most lasting achievements of the Anasazi are their cliff dwellings, sometimes built high on canyon walls, and their villages, called *pueblos*.

Directions: Use research materials and the information above to answer the following questions on your own paper.

1. Where did the Anasazi live?

2. What were the differences between the Basket Makers and the Anasazi?

3. When did the Anasazi culture develop?

4. What were the most lasting achievements of the Anasazi?

5. Why do you think the Anasazi built their houses facing south (think about the climate)?

6. Research and list at least two places you could see Anasazi architecture today.

The Ancient Americas   *Reproducibles*

Anasazi: Pithouse and Kiva

Name: _____ Date: _____

Directions: Read the text below, then follow the directions. When you are finished, show your model to your teacher to earn a puzzle piece.

The early Anasazi lived in pithouses. To make a pithouse, the Anasazi first dug a round hole, about four feet (122 cm) deep. Then, they placed four upright poles in the pit—these would be supports for the roof. After leaning posts against these supports, the Anasazi covered the outside with branches, grass, tree bark, and finally with a layer of clay.

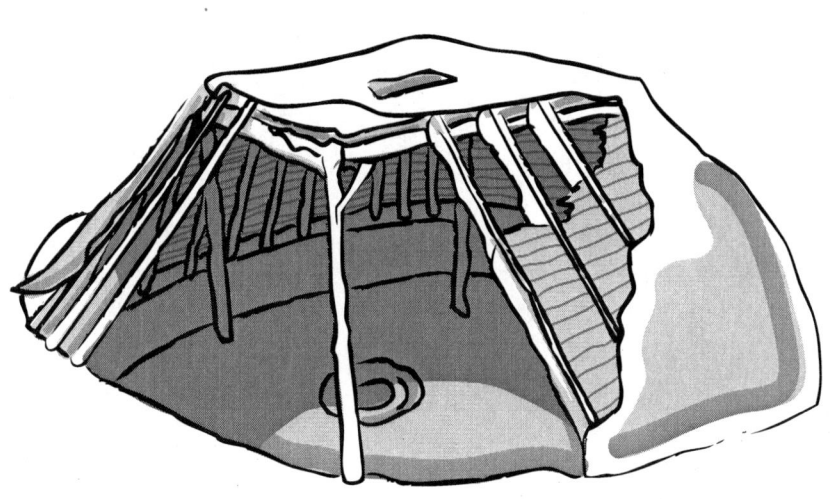

Later, the Anasazi moved their living quarters above ground. They sunk their religious structures, called kivas, even deeper into the earth. A kiva was a round chamber built underground that had a hole in the roof that people climbed through using a ladder. In the center of the kiva was a fireplace, and there was also a small hole in the floor, called a sipapu, which showed the people's connection with Mother Earth. Most communities had a kiva where people would go to discuss important matters facing the village.

Directions: Use craft materials and work with a partner to make a model of either a pithouse or a kiva. Take care in your construction—if your teacher can't tell which one you made, you will have to keep working.

The Ancient Americas *Reproducibles*

Anasazi: Pueblo

Name: _____ Date: _____

Directions: Read the text below, then follow the directions. When you are finished, show your project to your teacher to earn a puzzle piece.

The year A.D. 750 marks the start of the pueblo period, in which the Anasazi built elaborate communities. Pueblos were like modern apartment buildings, the biggest of which had about 1,800 rooms and housed around 3,000 people. In addition to living spaces, pueblos had a number of underground kivas, where family clans could gather for religious purposes.

Some pueblos were built high on the sides of cliffs, taking advantage of caves in the cliff wall. Sometimes the only way to get to these pueblos was to climb the cliff using small toeholds carved into the rock.

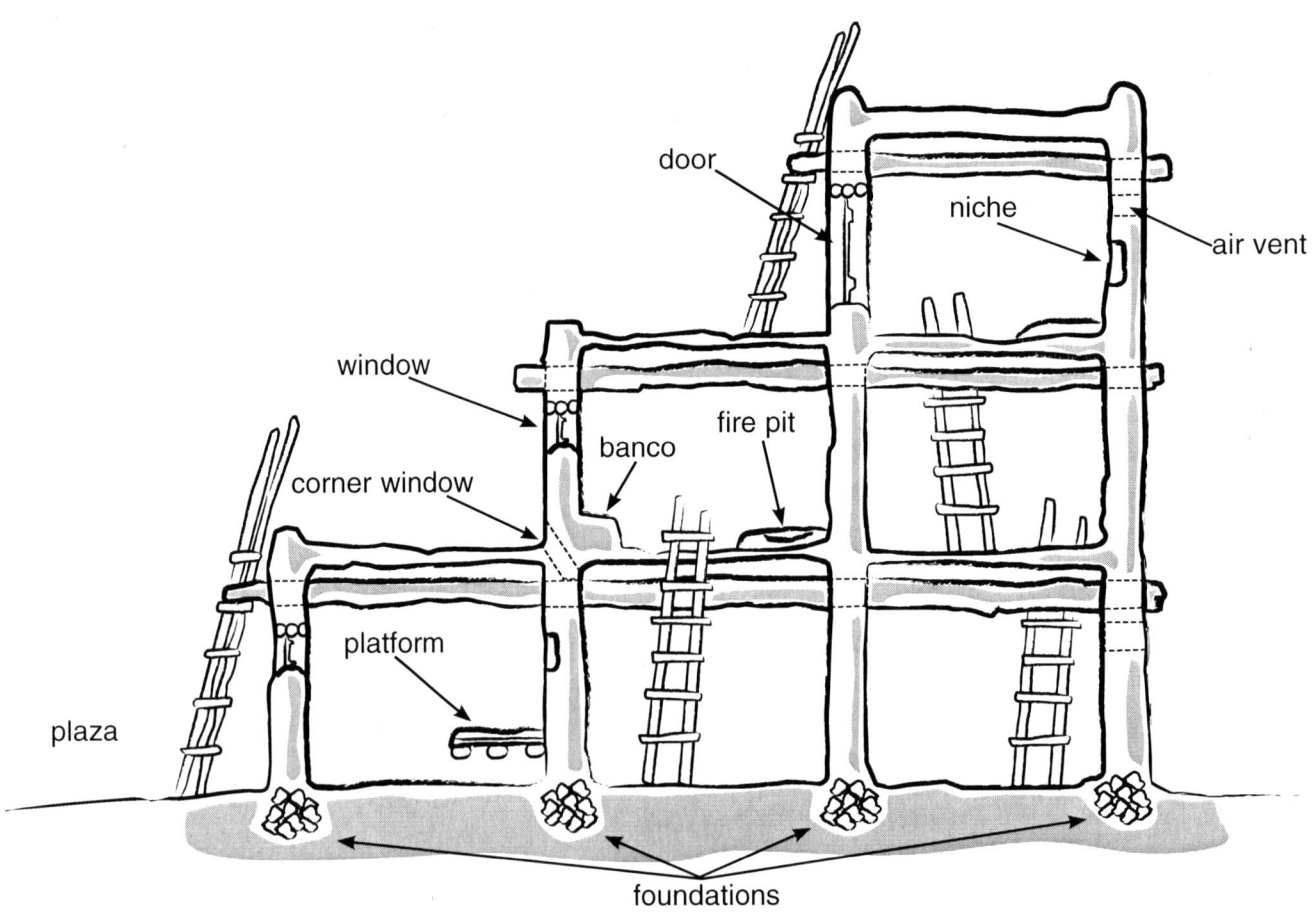

Directions: Work with a partner to make a poster showing an Anasazi pueblo. Label each part of your pueblo, and write a description of the history behind the pueblo period.

The Ancient Americas *Reproducibles*

Inca: Roads and Runners

Name: _____   Date: _____

Directions: Read the text below, then follow the directions. When you are finished, show your map to your teacher to earn a puzzle piece.

The Incas built a vast system of roads, over 14,000 miles (22.4 km) in all. There were two main roads, one that went north-south near the coast and another that ran north-south through the Andes Mountains. Many crossroads linked these two main roads. These roads allowed Inca rulers to control faraway places by quickly moving the military and by providing efficient communication. They also helped the Inca to transport building materials over great distances.

The Inca had a system of message runners who quickly carried information along the roads. There were messenger stations spaced every couple of miles, and when a runner neared the next station he would blow a shell trumpet, signaling the next runner to get ready. Like a relay race, messengers passed news from one to the next, and ensured that messages traveled as quickly as possible.

Directions: Work with a partner to make a map of the Inca Empire. Make sure you label the capital city of Cuzco and the Andes Mountains, and draw the two major roads. In a corner of your map, draw another small map of South America, showing how the Inca Empire fits on the continent. On the bottom of your map, write a short description about the Inca system of message runners. Use this outline as a guide to help you get started.

The Ancient Americas   Reproducibles

Inca: Stone Carving

Name: _____   Date: _____

Directions: Read the text below, then follow the directions. When you are finished, show your stone wall to your teacher to earn a puzzle piece.

The Incas were such expert stone carvers that their stone buildings fit together perfectly like puzzle pieces, without needing to be held together by mortar. It seems like a building without mortar would be less strong, but when there was an earthquake, the Inca stone walls wobbled and then fell right back into place, instead of cracking and falling like the walls that depend on mortar.

Unlike most civilizations that built stone walls, the Incas didn't use square blocks. Instead, they left the rock as close to its original shape as possible, just flattening out the sides needed to make them fit. In the picture below, you can see how many irregular blocks sit together perfectly. It's said that Inca stonework was so tight that you couldn't even fit a sheet of paper between the blocks.

Source: The Library of Congress

Directions: Work with a partner to create an Incan stone wall. Start with a bar of soap. Cut it into blocks, and then carve these blocks so they fit together to make a wall. Your stone wall needs to include at least five separate blocks. Mount your wall on a cardboard base.

The Ancient Americas   Reproducibles

Inca: End of the Empire

Name: _____   Date: _____

Directions: Read the text below, then follow the directions. When you are finished, show your answers to your teacher to earn a puzzle piece.

In 1532, Francisco Pizarro and his group of 180 conquistadores arrived in South America from Spain. The Inca Empire was threatened for the first time. Pizarro arranged a peaceful meeting with the Inca ruler, Atahualpa, but instead of deciding how to live in peace, Pizarro kidnapped Atahualpa and held him for ransom. The Inca were forced to pay $50 million in gold for their ruler's release. After getting the money, the Spanish decided to kill Atahualpa anyway. Then, the conquistadores marched straight toward the capital city of Cuzco.

Once the conquistadores sent gold back to Spain, reinforcements soon arrived. Pizarro still had only 400 soldiers to the Incan 40,000, but was able to defeat the Incas for the following three reasons:

1. Many of the Incan warriors died of the disease smallpox, which was brought to them by the Spanish conquistadores. Smallpox killed two out of every three Incans.

2. The conquistadors were able to convince tribes under Incan rule to help them overthrow the Incas.

3. While the weapons of the Incas were effective in tribal warfare, they were no match for the guns of the conquistadores.

However, the conquistadores weren't able to completely wipe out the Incas. A group of Incan warriors retreated to the mountain city of Machu Picchu, where they had no contact with Western society until they were discovered by Hiram Bingham in 1911. Machu Picchu was built to honor the sun god, the most important of all the Incan gods.

Directions: Use the information above and research materials to answer the following questions on your own paper.

1. In what year did Francisco Pizarro arrive in South America?
2. How did dishonesty help the conquistadores conquer the Incas?
3. What is the name of the city where the last of the Incan warriors fled?
4. What is the name of the disease that killed 2/3 of the Incan population?
5. What was the capital city of the Incan Empire?
6. How do you think the world would be different if the Incas had been immune to the disease you listed in question 4?

©Shell Educational Publishing

The Ancient Americas   *Reproducibles*

Inca: Terraced Farming

Name: _____ Date: _____

Directions: Read the text below, then follow the directions. When you are finished, show your model to your teacher to earn a puzzle piece.

The Andes Mountains are second only to the Himalayas in altitude. The Incas, who lived in the Andes, didn't have open fields to farm and had to learn new farming techniques that worked in the mountains.

Most importantly, they had to solve the problem of soil erosion—if the Incas farmed on steep hillsides, all the good soil would wash toward the bottom of the hills as it rained. To solve the problem of soil erosion, the Incas developed terraced agriculture. The Incas carved the hillside into a series of flat steps. Each step was reinforced with a stone wall. In this way, the Incas took sloping ground and made many stairs of flat ground, which wouldn't wash away.

The Incas also created a system of irrigation ditches to carry water to dry regions. Instead of using stone, which cracked, or sand, which let the water escape, the Incas used clay to line their irrigation ditches. The clay soaked up just enough moisture to avoid cracking, while keeping the water inside the ditch.

Directions: Look at the picture of terraced farming below. Work with a partner and use craft materials to create a model of terraced farming. Mount your model on cardboard, and write a description of terraced farming on the base.

Source: Kim Copeland

The Ancient Americas *Reproducibles*

Inca: Quipus

Name: _____ Date: _____

Directions: Read the text below, then follow the directions. When you are finished, show your *quipu* to your teacher to earn a puzzle piece.

The Incas didn't have writing and had to find another way to record information. They especially needed a way to record what was going on in far provinces of the empire so that messengers wouldn't get the information mixed up. Rulers needed information about the army, food, gold, population, and time.

The tool the Incas invented to record this information is called a *quipu*. On a *quipu*, various colors of string meant different things. For example, the thread that told how much gold a province had was yellow, the army thread was red, and the amount of food a province had could be green. In each thread, the Incas tied knots to tell how much of each of these things they had. The furthest knots from the center represented ones, the next knots were tens, etc. For example, on the second string of the *quipu* below, there are four knots at the bottom and one knot closer in—thus, there is one "ten" and four "ones," which makes 14.

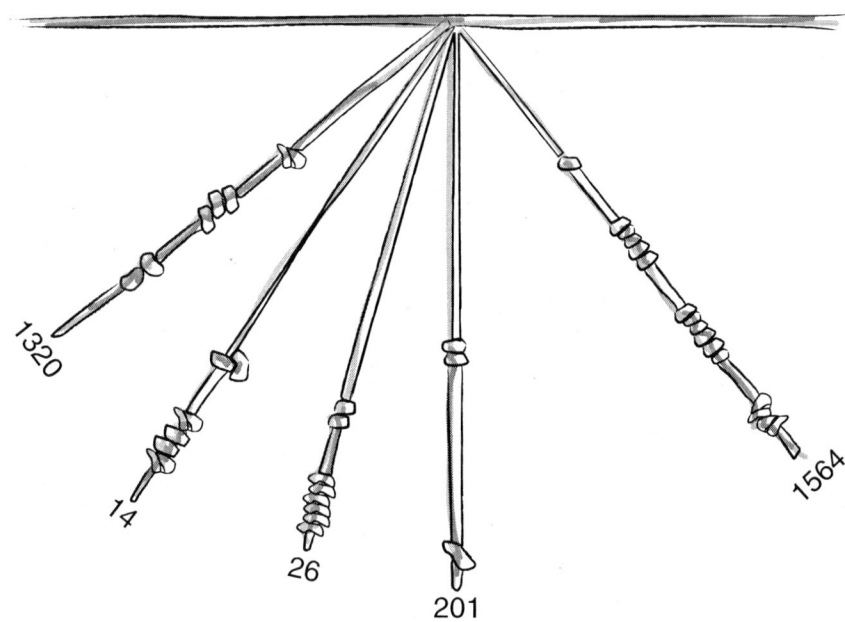

Directions: Work with a partner to create a *quipu*. First, pick three colors to represent different things. For example, you might choose green to represent the number of cents in your pocket or blue to represent how many hours are left until school is out. Next, create your *quipu*—tie three colored strings (or use pens to create colored string) to a higher string as in the picture above. Tie knots in your colored strings to show how many of each of these things there are. Write an explanation for your *quipu*.

©Shell Educational Publishing   69   #9357 Hands-on History: World History Activities

The Ancient Americas *Reproducibles*

Aztec: Goddess Myth

Name: _____ Date: _____

Directions: Below is the Aztec creation myth. Work with a partner or in a group of three to make an illustrated book of this myth. Your book needs to include at least four colorful illustrations. When you are finished, show it to your teacher to earn a puzzle piece.

Quetzalcoatl, the feathered serpent god and ruler of the sky, and Tezcatlipoca, magician god of the night, sat in the heavens creating people and sending them down to the water-covered earth below. There was no land, only a gigantic goddess floating upon the waters, eating everything with her many mouths. Every time Quetzalcoatl or Tezcatlipoca created a person, the goddess would swallow it up.

The two gods liked the people they created and didn't want them eaten by the goddess, so they transformed themselves into two huge serpents and descended into the water. One of them grabbed the goddess by the arms while the other grabbed her around the legs, and before she could resist, they pulled until she broke apart.

Her head and shoulders became the earth and the lower part of her body the sky.

The other gods were angry at what Quetzalcoatl and Tezcatlipoca had done and felt badly for the goddess. The other gods decided to let the goddess provide all the things people needed to survive—from her hair they created trees, grass, and flowers. Caves, fountains, and wells came from her eyes; rivers from her mouth; hills and valleys from her nose; and mountains from her shoulders.

Still the goddess was often sad, and the people could hear her crying in the night.

They knew she wept because of her thirst for human blood and that she would not provide food from the soil until she drank blood.

So the Aztecs gave the goddess the gift of human hearts.

The goddess who provides everything needed for human life also demands human life. So it has always been; so it will ever be.

The Ancient Americas   *Reproducibles*

Aztec: Floating Gardens

Name: _____   Date: _____

Directions: Read the text below, then follow the directions. When you are finished, show your teacher your poster to earn a puzzle piece.

The Aztecs built their great city of Tenochtitlan in the middle of a swamp. The city was surrounded on all sides by water, which made it easy to defend, but it was not so easy to farm in the swamp. To get more usable farmland, the Aztecs created floating farms called chinampas.

First, they wove together the trunks of many trees, which floated on the water. Then, they covered this floating mat with soil, which they dredged from the bottom of the swamp in order to create canals where ships could pass. This soil was rich in nutrients, and the Aztecs were frequently able to grow a surplus of corn, squash, and beans. Chinampas were kept from drifting away by driving huge stakes into the muck or by planting trees in the swamp that grew up through the chinampa and held it in place. Eventually, a chinampa could become a small island.

At its height, 300,000 people lived in Tenochtitlan, and crops grown on chinampas made up one-half to two-thirds of the food eaten by the people of the city.

Directions: Work in a group of two or three students to make a poster describing an Aztec chinampa. Your poster needs to be colorful and needs to include a written description of each part of your chinampa and how it was used in Aztec times.

The Ancient Americas *Reproducibles*

Aztec: Founding Myth

Name: _____ Date: _____

Directions: Answer the questions below. When you are finished, show your answers to your teacher to earn a puzzle piece.

Question 1: Work by yourself and use research materials to search the flags of the world. On which flag is there a picture of an eagle with a snake in its mouth, sitting on a cactus (as shown below)? Clue: This flag is red, green, and white.

_____

Legend says that the Aztec people were forced from their homes and wandered for hundreds of years looking for a new place to settle. The god Huitzilopochtli told the Aztec people that when they saw an eagle sitting on a cactus with a snake in its mouth, they would know they had found the right place to build a great city. Many times, the Aztecs came across a promising location, but they failed to find the sign and they kept searching. Finally in A.D. 1325, they found themselves on the shores of Lake Texcoco. The lake was swampy and mosquito-infested, and the Aztecs were about to move on when one warrior with keen eyes stood and pointed toward the center of the lake. There on a rocky island, grew a prickly-pear cactus and on this cactus sat an eagle with a live snake in its mouth. The Aztecs had found the sign! Though it seemed strange to build a city in the middle of a swamp, they didn't question the wisdom of Huitzilopochtli. The Aztecs named their great city Tenochtitlan, which means "place where cactus grows from stone."

Question 2: A modern city was built on the ruins of Tenochtitlan. This city is the capital of the country you listed in the first question. Use research materials to discover the name of this city.

_____

Question 3: Do you think the Aztecs were right to follow the advice of Huitzilopochtli? Why or why not? Write on the back of this page if you need more space for your answer.

_____

_____

#9357 *Hands-on History: World History Activities* ©*Shell Educational Publishing*

The Ancient Americas   *Reproducibles*

Aztec: Codex

Name: _____   Date: _____

Directions: Complete this task before working on *Aztec: Writing*. When you are finished, show your codex to your teacher to earn a puzzle piece.

Unlike the Mayas, the Aztecs used a system of writing to keep track of the workings of the empire. A ruler named Xtiuxochiti described the things that Aztec scribes would have written:

"They had scribes for each branch of knowledge. Some dealt with the annals, putting down in order the things that happened each year, giving the day, month, and hour. Others had charge of the genealogies, recording the lineage of rulers, lords and noblemen, registering the newborn and deleting those who had died."

At the height of Aztec civilization, the city of Tenochtitlan used more than 480,000 sheets of paper per year, which were made into a type of scroll called a codex. Of these many, many codices that were made, only a few still exist. The Spanish conquistadors destroyed most, and the ones that the Aztecs hid rotted due to the area's humid climate.

Each codex was made from a long strip of paper, which was about six to seven inches wide and sometimes up to 13 yards (11.8 m) long. This long piece of paper was folded like an accordion or zigzag and once it was all folded, the Aztecs used a wood cover for both the front and the back.

Directions: Work with a partner and use cardboard, paper, tape, and glue to create an Aztec codex as described below.

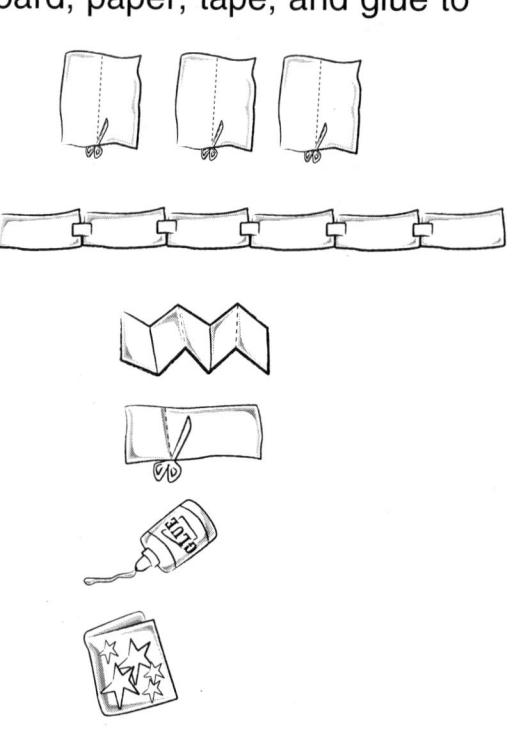

1. Cut three sheets of regular letter-sized paper in half across the middle.

2. Using as little tape as possible, tape them back together to form a long sheet that is 5.5 inches (14 cm) wide.

3. Fold this long sheet in a zigzag pattern along the lines you taped.

4. Cut out cardboard to use as a front cover and a back cover.

5. Use glue to attach your covers.

6. Decorate the covers of your codex.

©Shell Educational Publishing   73   #9357 *Hands-on History: World History Activities*

The Ancient Americas   Reproducibles

Aztec: Writing

Name: _____   Date: _____

Directions: Complete the *Aztec: Codex* sheet before starting this one. When you finish this sheet, show it to your teacher to earn a puzzle piece.

Aztec writing looked similar to Egyptian hieroglyphics, but it could sometimes be interpreted in different ways. For example, if you drew an eye, it could be a pictogram (meaning an eye as part of the body), it could be an ideogram (meaning the idea of sight), or it could be phonetic (meaning the sound "I"). This could make reading Aztec writing a bit difficult, and the people went to many years of school before they were able to read.

Writing was a two-person job for the Aztecs. First, a scribe would write the black outlines of all the symbols, and then a painter would fill in the symbols with red, blue, green, and yellow paints.

Directions: On a separate piece of paper, work with a partner to make up your own symbols for at least 20 things, ideas, actions, or places. Use the examples in the box below to help you. Draw your symbols on the pages of the codex you made earlier. Also, write an Aztec name for each symbol and the symbol's English translation. Don't forget to color your symbols using red, blue, green, and yellow. After you have created your 20 symbols, use them to write a sentence. Be creative!

Remember: The Aztecs wrote in columns instead of in lines. They read from the top down.

#9357 Hands-on History: World History Activities   ©Shell Educational Publishing

The Ancient Americas   *Reproducibles*

Map Evaluation

Name: _____ Date: _____

Look at your finished puzzle to answer the questions below. When you are finished with this sheet, you have finished the activity!

1. What three things do you see that look like especially smart designs?

   _____

   _____

   _____

2. What challenges did this society's architects face?

   _____

   _____

3. List one thing about this city/architecture that you think is unique.

   _____

4. If you had to split this city in four "sections," what would they be? What would each section be used for, and what would they be called?

   _____

   _____

   _____

   _____

5. What type of people do you think lived in this city? How can you tell?

   _____

   _____

6. List three things you notice about this map that you think other students might miss.

   _____

   _____

   _____

The Ancient Americas   *Reproducibles*

Ancient Americas Quiz

Name: _____ Date: _____

Directions: Circle the best answer to each question below.

1. Which of the following cultures did not live in Ancient America?
   - A. Aztec
   - B. Maya
   - C. Visigoths
   - D. Anasazi

2. Which of the following societies built cliff dwellings in the U.S. Southwest?
   - A. Aztec
   - B. Maya
   - C. Visigoths
   - D. Anasazi

3. Which culture created the city of Tenochtitlan?
   - A. Aztec
   - B. Maya
   - C. Inca
   - D. Anasazi

4. Which culture created the city of Machu Picchu?
   - A. Aztec
   - B. Maya
   - C. Inca
   - D. Anasazi

5. Which culture created the city of Tikal?
   - A. Aztec
   - B. Maya
   - C. Inca
   - D. Anasazi

6. Which culture created pueblos?
   - A. Aztec
   - B. Maya
   - C. Inca
   - D. Anasazi

7. Describe one of the following, including at least five details: Tikal, Machu Picchu, Tenochtitlan, or a pueblo.

_____

_____

_____

_____

_____

Habits of Mind Discussion

- Which of the four civilizations we studied in this unit do you think was the most advanced? Why?

- What are the similarities among these four societies?

- What are the major differences among these four societies?

- How do you think history would be different if members of these societies were immune to the disease smallpox?

- Which of these four societies do you think is most like ours? Why?

- How much do you think we can learn about a culture by studying its architecture? Is architecture the most important measure of a society?

Civilizations of Asia   Lesson Plans

Civilizations of Asia

Overview

On three successive days, students will split into groups and complete tasks representing religion, government, and mythology. After each day, students will enter the information they find on a cardboard wheel, with the three types of tasks able to spin independently of each other. Once students have completed their tasks and have entered the information on the wheel, they will try to spin the dials of the wheel to match the correct information with India, China, and Japan, earning a classroom reward of your choice if they are correct. This activity promotes animated discussion and learning through discourse.

You will measure student learning through discussion and an end-of-activity quiz.

Example of a Hindu Temple
Source: Gillian Eve Makepeace

Objectives

- Students will explain how societies act differently based on their shared assumptions, values, and beliefs. (NCSS)
- Students will learn how religion, government, and daily life interact to create the cultures of India, China, and Japan.

Materials

- copies of reproducibles (pages 84–110) as described on page 79
- large sheet of butcher or poster paper, at least 3' x 3' (91 cm x 91 cm)
- one sheet of cardboard the same size as your poster/butcher paper
- two 2' x 2' (61 cm x 61 cm) sheets of cardboard
- popsicle sticks
- salt dough or clay

Civilizations of Asia   Lesson Plans

Civilizations of Asia (cont.)

Preparation

Total preparation time should be about 30 minutes.

1. Create the Information Wheel as shown on pages 84–85. Alternately, you can copy these directions and have students complete this wheel as their first task.
2. Make one copy of each religion, government, and mythology sheet (pages 86–108).
3. Make a class set of *Civilizations of Asia Quiz* (page 109).
4. Make an overhead of the *Habits of Mind Discussion* (page 110).

Directions

1. This activity will take a total of four days, with one day spent on religion, one on government, one on mythology, and one on discussion and wrap-up.

2. After reading the *Read-Aloud Directions* (pages 80–81), split students into three groups and give each group one of the three religion sheets. Allow the remainder of the period for completion, closing with the short *Day 1 Discussion* (page 81). Don't forget to tell students when there are ten minutes left in the period, at which time they should transfer their information to the appropriate place on the Information Wheel and clean up.

3. At the beginning of the second day, split students into three groups (not necessarily the same groups as yesterday). Distribute the government sheets, and allow students time to work. Stop the activity with 15 minutes remaining. Have students transfer their information to the Information Wheel. Have them clean quietly while you close the class with the short *Day 2 Discussion* (page 81).

4. As you did the previous two days, split students into new groups. Then, distribute the mythology sheets and allow time for completion. Have students transfer their information to the Information Wheel. Close with the short *Day 3 Discussion* (page 81).

5. Move the Information Wheel to the front of the class. Have student volunteers spin the discs of the wheel until they think they have matched the society with the correct religion/government/daily life. Discuss throughout the activity why students think these parameters match. Focus your discussion especially on how these three aspects cannot necessarily be separated and how each affects the others.

6. Close with the *Habits of Mind Discussion* and give the *Civilizations of Asia Quiz*.

Things to Consider

1. Unlike other activities in this book, students will not be keeping the same groups throughout. This may cause some confusion at first, so be sure to prepare students and treat each day as its own independent mini-activity.

Civilizations of Asia (cont.)

Things to Consider (cont.)

2. Because group sizes are large (each is one-third of the class), you may find that only certain students are doing the majority of the work; combat this situation by asking groups to preplan who will be doing what.
3. By correctly matching the ideas on the Information Wheel with the appropriate country, students will earn a classroom reward of your choice. The larger the reward, the more motivation students will have during the activity.
4. Some sheets are more difficult than others, and you might want to assign more students to these groups. Difficult tasks include the following:
   - *Religion: Hinduism/Islam*
   - *Mythology Three*

Read-Aloud Directions

What is the most important part of a society? Is it the religion, the government, the mythology . . . what? Imagine you lived in medieval Asia, where China, Japan, and India each had its own religion, government, and mythology. If you lived in one of these countries, would your mythology be different if you had different beliefs? How about your government—how could your religion affect the government you choose?

For the next few days, we will try to answer these questions. Today, we will look at religion. Tomorrow, we will explore government, and the next day we will look at mythology. At first you won't know which country your ideas are from, but once we have gathered all the information we need, we will try to match the ideas with the correct country. If you can match things up just right, you will earn *[insert classroom reward of your choice].*

Here's how it will work:

For the next couple of days, I will be splitting you into three groups and giving each group a sheet that explains tasks to be completed. The groups will not be the same every day, so you will get the opportunity to work with different people and might end up working on the religion sheet that matches India, the government sheet that matches China, and the mythology sheet that happens to match Japan. At the end of the period, you will write the information you learn in a slot of the Information Wheel *[preview the wheel].* Once you have completed all your tasks and entered the information on the wheel, you will try to turn the discs of the Information Wheel so that all three ideas match the correct country.

Civilizations of Asia (cont.)

> **Read-Aloud Directions** (cont.)
>
> The better the information you write on the Information Wheel, the easier it will be to make the correct matches, and the easier it will be to earn *[insert the classroom reward of your choice]*. Good Luck!
>
> *[Place students in three groups, distribute religion sheets, and begin the activity.]*

Daily Discussions

Day 1 Discussion

Discuss the similarities and differences among the religions of Hinduism, Islam, Shintoism, and Confucianism (which is technically a way of thought, not a religion). Also, help students see that a culture that follows any of these religions is likely to have certain values. Islam and Hinduism are presented on one sheet because they were both present in one of the Asian societies of this unit. Based on the religions, how well do students think these religious groups got along?

Day 2 Discussion

Again, help students make distinctions between these three forms of government (empire, dynasty, and feudalism), and also start to explore which religions are likely to fit with these styles of government. There are many similarities between these three styles of government (many include hereditary passing of power), but help students see that underneath the emperor/king/ruler, the governments are very different.

Day 3 Discussion

What do these stories say about the cultures that created them? What do these cultures value? You may even have students present the illustrated books they created and explain the answers they wrote on the Information Wheel.

Civilizations of Asia (cont.)

Answer Key

Information Wheel Answers

Japan: Shintoism, Feudalism, Mythology One
China: Confucianism, Dynasty, Mythology Three
India: Hinduism/Islam, Empire, Mythology Two

Religion: Hinduism/Islam (pages 86–89)

Students should create models of the Hindu Gods Brahma, Vishnu, Shiva, and Ganesha and should write short descriptions of each god on a cardboard base. Students should also create Muslim prayer mats as well as posters showing the Five Pillars of Islam.

1. Hindus believe in many gods.
2. Muslims believe in only one god.
3. Hindus think that one must be born Hindu and cannot be converted to the religion.
4. Iman (faith), Salah (prayer), Zakah (giving), Sawn (fasting), and Hajj (pilgrimage)
5. Brahma (creator), Vishnu (maintainer), Shiva (destroyer), and sometimes Ganesha (remover of obstacles)

Religion: Confucianism (pages 90–91)

1. Confucianism is not a religion; it is a code of conduct for everyday life.
2. Li: Rules of respect, ritual, and etiquette; Hsiao: Family love; Yi: Righteousness; Xin: Honesty and trustworthiness; Jen: Kindness toward others; and Chung: Loyalty to the government
3. A philosopher and teacher
4. "Do unto others as you would have them do unto you."
5. Jobs were based on merit.

Religion: Shintoism (pages 92–93)

1. There is no founder or holy book.
2. Ancestors and nature. Other answers include "Kami."
3. Objects in nature, ancestors, heroes, rulers, animals, etc.
4. Tradition and family, love of nature, physical cleanliness, and matsuri (rituals)
5. Answers can include the following: matsuri (rituals), tori (sacred temple gates), Kami (gods), or goshintai (god-body or altar).

Government: Empire (pages 94–96)

Akbar is considered this empire's greatest ruler.

1. Students should list and describe Akbar, Babar, Aurangzeb, and Shah Jahan.
2. The strength of an empire depends on the competence of the ruler.
3. Answers can include religious tolerance, taxation, emphasis on military, emphasis on arts and architecture, etc.
4. Answers can include a dwindling treasury, threat from local governors of internal war, threats from outside borders, etc.

Civilizations of Asia (cont.)

Answer Key (cont.)

Government: Dynasties (pages 97–99)

Due to its arts and culture, the Tang dynasty is considered the golden age of this civilization, though the Song dynasty is also sometimes considered part of this golden age as well.

1. Tang: arts; Song: economy and cities; Ming: trade and exploration
2. In a dynasty, power is passed down within a family.
3. Government officials were chosen by merit.

Government: Feudalism (pages 100–103)

The chart should be in the following order, starting at the top: Emperor, Shogun, Diamyos, Samuri, Ronin, Peasants, Artisans, Merchants.

Mythology One (page 104)

1. Answers should include three of the following: Sun Goddess, Rock Princess, Flower Princess, blooming trees, God (Kami) of the land.
2. This myth shows that the culture in question believes that all things are impermanent.
3. Answers will vary and can include respect within family, beauty, wisdom, and non-attachment.

Mythology Two (page 105)

1. Ganesha is an elephant.
2. Ganesha is the remover of obstacles.
3. Answers will vary but should include something about refraining from vanity and ego.

Mythology Three (pages 106–108)

1. The poor couple believes that their son can improve his station in life.
2. The frog earns his position in government through intelligence and honesty.
3. The emperor was dishonest—he went back on his word to wed his daughter to whomever could drive away the invaders.
4. This society probably does not respect women as equals because the family believes that only a boy can earn his way out of poverty, and the emperor does not ask his daughter's advice concerning whom she should marry.

Civilizations of Asia Quiz (page 109)

1.

	Government	Religion	Myth
India	Empire	Hindu/Islam	The Story of Gajamugasuran
China	Dynasty	Confucianism	The Frog Who Became an Emperor
Japan	Feudalism	Shintoism	Flower Princess and Rock Princess

2. Answers will vary. Students should write two facts about each religion.
3. Answers will vary. Students should write two facts about each form of government.

Civilizations of Asia — *Reproducibles*

Information Wheel Construction Directions

1. Cut four cardboard discs of approximately the following radii: 2 feet (61 cm), 1.5 feet (46 cm), 1 foot (30 cm), and 0.5 feet (15 cm).

2. Draw lines that split each disc into thirds.

3. Stack the discs, and push a bendable brad through the middle of all the discs such that each disc can spin independently of the others (or you can mount the Information Wheel on the wall and drive a large pushpin/nail through the center).

4. Label the three spaces of the innermost disc *India*, *China*, and *Japan*.

5. Label the three spaces of the next disc *Confucianism*, *Shintoism*, and *Hinduism/Islam*.

6. Label the three spaces of the next disc *Feudalism*, *Empire*, and *Dynasty*.

7. Label the three spaces of the largest disc *Mythology One*, *Mythology Two*, and *Mythology Three*.

8. It is important to label the spaces exactly as shown, or they might not match up later on.

9. Use the diagram on page 85 to check the construction of your Information Wheel.

Civilizations of Asia *Reproducibles*

Information Wheel Construction Diagram

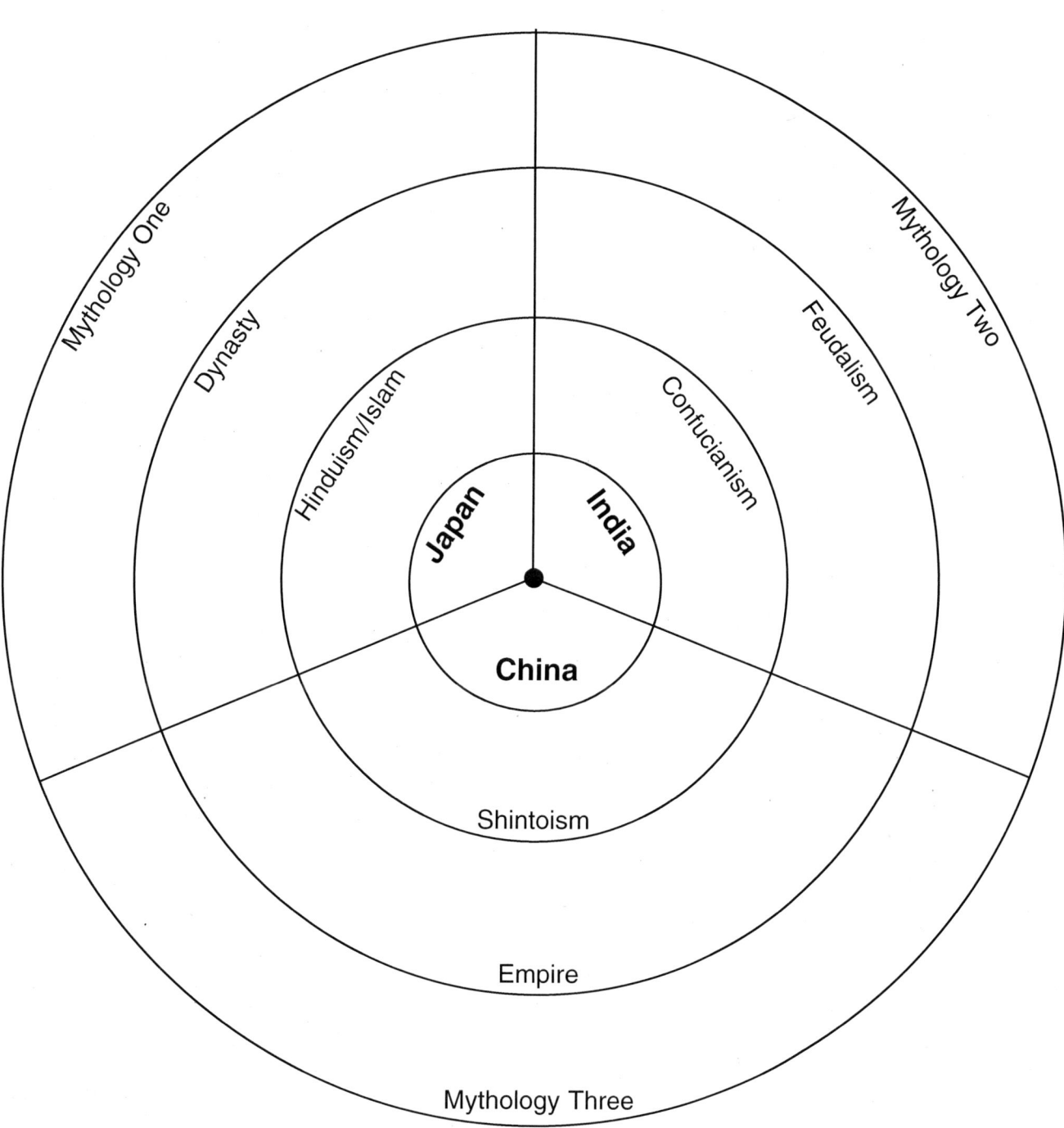

Civilizations of Asia   *Reproducibles*

Religion: Hinduism/Islam

Names: _____ Date: _____

In one of the Asian civilizations you are studying, the ruling class was Islamic and the common people were mostly Hindu. Sometimes the Hindu people were required to pay more tax than the Muslims (Islamic people). The golden age of this civilization was the time in which Muslims and Hindus got along. During this period, the civilization could put more energy into art, architecture, learning, and culture without having to spend time and money making sure the people didn't fight each other.

Directions: Read the information on the next four pages and then complete the activities. When you have finished the activities, answer the questions and write these answers in the space on the Information Wheel marked *Hinduism/Islam*.

Hinduism

There are three main Hindu Gods: Brahma (the creator), Vishnu (the maintainer), and Shiva (the destroyer). In addition to these three gods, Ganesha is also important.

Activity: Use craft materials to make models of these gods. Mount each model on a base, and write a short description of the god and his duties.

Brahma: Brahma has four heads—one to watch over each of the four directions (north, south, east, and west). Frequently, Brahma is shown sitting on a lotus and holding the Vedas (holy book), which Hindus believe he gave to Earth. Brahma is the god who creates souls and sets them on the path of birth, death, and rebirth (reincarnation). Hindus believe that unless you are born a Hindu (and created by Brahma), you can't become a Hindu. Because you can't become a Hindu later in life, the Hindu people didn't try to conquer non-Hindus in hopes of converting them.

Brahma

Religion: Hinduism/Islam (cont.)

Vishnu: Vishnu is the maintainer of Earth and the god of everyday life. When people are in trouble, Vishnu takes on an animal form and comes to their rescue. Usually, Vishnu is shown as a blue god who holds the chakra (energy), conch shell, lotus, and a mace in his four hands.

Shiva: Shiva is the god of destruction but also the god of knowledge; he wears a necklace of skulls but he is not all bad. Hindus believe that without destruction, there can be no creation and that death/destruction is a natural part of life. Shiva is usually shown sitting in meditation with his eyes half closed, and he usually wears a leopard skin.

Vishnu

Shiva

Ganesha: Though Ganesha is not one of the three main gods, he is the most widely worshipped. Ganesha has the power to remove all obstacles, so Hindu people frequently pray to Ganesha when they undertake a task. As you can see, Ganesha is shown as an elephant.

Ganesha

Religion: Hinduism/Islam (cont.)

Islam

Islamic people (called Muslims) follow the Five Pillars of Islam: Iman (faith), Salah (prayer), Zakah (giving), Sawn (fasting), and Hajj (pilgrimage).

Iman: Islam was founded by the prophet Mohammed, who was born in A.D. 570. At this time, the people in Mohammed's area worshipped many gods. So, it was important for the followers of Mohammed to say, "There is none worthy of worship except God, and Mohammed is the messenger of God." This phrase is still the most important expression of Iman (faith) used by Muslims today.

Remember this phrase, and write it at the top of the prayer mat you will make in the next task.

Salah: Muslim people pray five times a day, always pointing east toward the sacred mosque called Haram Sharif, which is in the city of Mecca. When Muslim people pray, they kneel on a special mat which they usually carry with them.

Activity: Cut open paper bags and tape them together to form a prayer mat that is big enough to kneel on. Decorate your prayer mat similar to the one shown in the picture, and write the prayer from Iman on your mat (don't forget to draw a compass so that people using your mat will always know which way is east!).

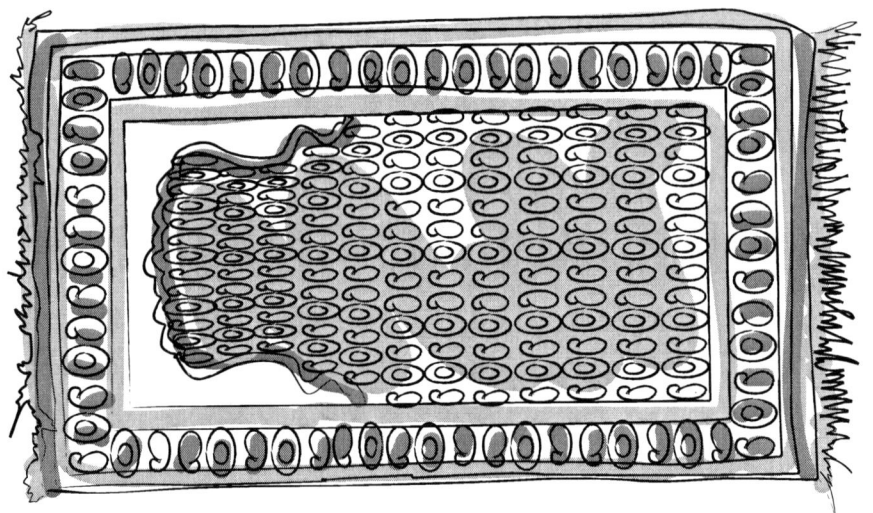

Zakah: Muslim people are required by their faith to give 1/40 of their wealth to charity. If people cannot pay, they may give something they made, or if they are truly poor, they may refrain from doing evil acts, which Mohammed said is also an act of charity.

Activity: Spend five minutes right now helping to clean the classroom. This is your charitable act.

Civilizations of Asia   *Reproducibles*

Religion: Hinduism/Islam *(cont.)*

Sawn: During the holy month of Ramadan, Muslims don't eat between the hours of sunup and sundown. This fasting is supposed to help Muslim people stay constantly aware of the presence of God.

Hajj: Muhammad said that every Muslim who is able should make a pilgrimage, or Hajj, to the holy city of Mecca.

Activity: Work with the people of your group to make a poster showing the Five Pillars of Islam, including a small map that shows Mecca (use research materials to find Mecca).

Questions: Write the answers to these questions here. Then, transfer them to the Information Wheel in the spot marked *Hinduism/Islam*.

1. In how many gods do Hindus believe?

   _____

2. In how many gods do Muslims believe?

   _____

3. Why did Hindus not try to convert the people around them?

   _____

4. What are the Five Pillars of Islam?

   _____

   _____

   _____

   _____

   _____

5. Who are the main Hindu gods and what do they do?

   _____

   _____

   _____

Civilizations of Asia   *Reproducibles*

Religion: Confucianism

Names: _____ Date: _____

Directions: Read the information on the next two pages and then complete the activities. When you have finished the activities, answer the questions and write these answers in the space on the Information Wheel marked *Confucianism*.

Confucius was a great teacher and philosopher who lived during a time of great unrest. He traveled the countryside helping individuals to live better lives and rulers to use their powers more effectively. Confucius, like Jesus, believed the golden rule was "Do unto others as you would have them do unto you."

Confucianism isn't actually a religion—it's a code of conduct for daily life. For example, Confucianism doesn't say what happens when you die. Confucianism tells how the family should act when someone dies, but a Buddhist, Taoist, or even Christian minister might actually preside over the funeral. You can follow the teaching of Confucius while considering yourself a member of another religion.

However, Confucianism had a strong effect on one of the societies you are studying!

There are six values in Confucianism:

- **Li:** Rules of respect, ritual, and etiquette. Confucianism taught that people should be polite and should follow strict rules of social behavior.
- **Hsiao:** Family love, including the love of children for parents and parents for children
- **Yi:** Righteousness. People should act morally because it is the right thing to do, not just because they want to profit from it.
- **Xin:** Honesty and trustworthiness
- **Jen:** Kindness toward others. This is the most important rule of Confucianism.
- **Chung:** Loyalty to the government

Civilizations of Asia   *Reproducibles*

Religion: Confucianism *(cont.)*

Confucius also taught that the best qualified people should be chosen for government jobs, not necessarily the people who were from the best families. Jobs based on merit helped ensure that intelligent people ran the country.

Activity: For each of these values, write and illustrate a short story in which one or more of the characters displays this virtue. You can include all these stories in a book, or you can present them on a poster. In your group, figure out who will be working on each value.

Questions: Write the answers to these questions here. Then, transfer them to the Information Wheel in the spot marked *Confucianism*.

1. Describe Confucianism—is it a religion? If not, what is it?

   _____

   _____

2. What are the six values of Confucianism (list and describe each)?

   _____

   _____

   _____

   _____

   _____

   _____

3. Who was Confucius?

   _____

   _____

4. What is the Golden Rule of Confucianism?

   _____

5. In Confucianism, how were people chosen for government jobs?

   _____

   _____

Civilizations of Asia   *Reproducibles*

Religion: Shintoism

Names: _____ Date: _____

Directions: Read the information on the next two pages and then complete the activities. When you have finished the activities, answer the questions and write these answers in the space on the Information Wheel marked *Shintoism*.

Unlike other religions, Shintoism has no founder (like Jesus, Buddha, or Muhammad) and no formal holy book (like the Bible, Koran, or Torah). Shintoism is a loosely organized system of belief based on the worship of ancestors and of nature. Shinto gods are known as Kami and can be animals, objects, heroes, rulers, or guardians. Many people are both Shinto and Buddhist, and these people view the Buddha as a Kami. Shinto rituals are called *matsuri*, and are meant to continue the harmony of the universe.

Like Confucianism and Islam, Shintoism is based upon principles. These include:

- Tradition and family
- Love of nature
- Physical cleanliness
- Matsuri (rituals)

To the right is a picture of the Shinto Ise Shrine. Shinto shrines are usually quite simple and are built in groves of trees, which can be as sacred as the shrines themselves. At the temple gates, called tori, worshippers wash their hands and mouths with water before entering. Inside the temple, instead of an altar or picture of a god, the shrine contains a goshintai, or god-body, which is either a mirror or nothing at all, and shows worshippers the simplicity of god. Every 20 years, the Ise Shrine is torn down and rebuilt to show the impermanence of life.

Civilizations of Asia   *Reproducibles*

Religion: Shintoism *(cont.)*

Activity: Use popsicle sticks to create a model of the Ise Shrine. Make sure your model includes a grove of trees, tori, and a goshintai. Mount your model on a cardboard base, and write the four principles of Shintoism on this base.

Questions: Write the answers to these questions here. Then, transfer them to the Information Wheel in the spot marked *Shintoism*.

1. How is Shintoism different from Christianity, Judaism, Islam, and Buddhism?

   _____
   _____
   _____
   _____

2. What do Shinto people worship?

   _____
   _____

3. Describe the forms that a Kami might take.

   _____
   _____
   _____

4. What are the four principles of Shintoism?

   _____
   _____
   _____
   _____

5. List and define at least three non-English words that have to do with the Shinto faith.

   _____
   _____
   _____

Civilizations of Asia *Reproducibles*

Government: Empire

Names: _____ Date: _____

Directions: Read the information on the next three pages and then complete the activities. When you have finished the activities, answer the questions and write these answers in the space on the Information Wheel marked *Empire*.

One of the civilizations you are studying was organized as an empire. In an empire, one emperor rules over all the land. This emperor has the power to do whatever he or she wants. If the emperor is good, the empire can flourish, but if the ruler is bad, the empire is in trouble!

Activity
1. In your group, choose which people will work on each of the emperors listed below. Try to make the number of people in each group equal.
2. Each group will draw a picture of its emperor and write a short biography.
3. Get together with the rest of your group—your job is to argue that your emperor was the best of the four.
4. As a group, vote on which emperor you think was actually the best.

Akbar: Akbar was only 13 years old when he became *padshah* (ruler of the empire), and for the first part of his rule, he let the general Bairam Khan tell him what to do. Akbar put military governors called *mansabars* in charge of each province. These mansabars were responsible for local government, and if they mistreated the people, they were held personally accountable. A cruel mansabar could be put to death.

Akbar collected one-third of all profits from crops as tax, but unlike some of the other rulers, he taxed everybody equally—until Akbar's rule, people of other religions were taxed more heavily, and the nobility was not taxed at all. Akbar invited people of all religions to join the government and made sure that mansabars were the same religion as the people in the province they governed.

Though Akbar never learned to read or write, he invited many poets, artists, and musicians to live with him in the royal palace. Akbar also built many gardens, temples, and palaces.

Government: Empire (cont.)

Aurangzeb: Aurangzeb was a great military ruler and spent 26 years fighting to extend the borders of his kingdom. His army consisted of 500,000 people, 50,000 camels, and 30,000 war elephants. He achieved great victories in both the northwest and the northeast, and was successful in putting down the frequent uprisings of local governors. Under Aurangzeb, the empire reached its largest point. However, to pay for his military campaigns, he had to raise taxes from one-third to one-half of all profits made on land. Still, the treasury became smaller every day.

Aurangzeb was also a deeply religious man. He felt that his god was the only god. This led him to require people of other religions to pay more in tax. Aurangzeb also forbade people of other religions from holding important government offices.

Babar: When Babar's small army of 12,000 men defeated the much larger force of Ibrahim Lodi at the battle of Panipat, Babar became the first ruler of this empire. Babar was a military leader first and a governor second, sometimes ruling more "by the sword" than "by the pen." However, he loved architecture and music and spoke many languages. Under Babar, artisans built temples and palaces, and many public gardens were built for the enjoyment of the people.

Some evidence shows that Babar might have destroyed the temples of other religions and built new temples to his god. He was not tolerant of other religions and taxed those who worshipped other gods more heavily than those who worshipped his god.

Shah Jahan: Shah Jahan inherited a great empire, but did little to extend its boundaries. Though he was an able military commander, he was defeated as often as he won, especially in Deccan to the south.

Civilizations of Asia — *Reproducibles*

Government: Empire *(cont.)*

Shah Jahan *(cont.)*: The military was not the only thing on which Shah Jahan spent money. He also created the beautiful Taj Mahal, which is known as the most spectacular building of the empire. It took more than 1,000 elephants and 20,000 men over 20 years to build the Taj Mahal and cost much of the treasury. The Taj Mahal is a tomb for Shah Jahan's queen Mumtaz Mahal, whom he loved and respected. Many historians believe that Mumtaz was an important advisor in the government. She died while giving birth to their 14th child.

Shah Jahan was forced to raise taxes from one-third to one-half of the value of crops to try to pay for his expenses, and still the treasury lost money.

Questions: Write the answers to these questions here. Then, transfer them to the Information Wheel in the spot marked *Empire*.

1. List the four important rulers of this empire, and write a one-sentence description of each.

   _____
   _____
   _____
   _____

2. What is the danger in government by empire?

   _____

3. List two important differences among these emperors.

   _____
   _____

4. What dangers do you think this empire faced (name at least two)?

   _____
   _____

Civilizations of Asia   *Reproducibles*

Government: Dynasties

Names: _____ Date: _____

Directions: Read the information on the next three pages and then complete the activities. When you have finished the activities, answer the questions and write these answers in the space on the Information Wheel marked *Dynasties*.

In a dynasty, power is passed down within a family. This can be good, or it can be bad—if it's obvious who the next ruler is, people won't fight over power, but passing power down within a family doesn't always mean the most intelligent person gets the job.

Luckily, in the dynasties you are studying, there was also a way of thought that encouraged rulers to choose the most qualified people for government jobs, not necessarily the people who came from the best families.

Activity

1. In your group, choose which people will work on each of the dynasties listed below. Try to make the number of people in each group equal.
2. Each small group will draw a picture of its dynasty and write a short description.
3. Get together with the rest of your group—your job is to argue that your dynasty was the best of the three.
4. As a group, vote on which dynasty you think was actually the best.

Source: Clipart.com

Tang Dynasty: In the Tang dynasty, especially under Emperor Xuanzong, the arts flourished. Sculpture, painting, poetry, literature, music, and ceramics all reached their highest point. Most art was modeled after peaceful scenes in nature, and the goal was not to reproduce things exactly as they were, but to catch the emotion and rhythm of nature. Other important models for art were the horse and camel, which were important to the Tang dynasty because they provided the only means of fighting the nomadic tribes to the north.

During the Tang dynasty, the capital city of Chang'an was the most populous city anywhere. If you walked the streets in the capital, you would hear languages from all over the known world—merchants, scholars, and explorers all flocked to the Tang dynasty.

Government: Dynasties *(cont.)*

Song Dynasty: The Song dynasty is known for the growth of cities and the economy as well as for developments in printing and education. Before the Song, every book was copied by hand; this took a long time, and very few books were available. During the Song dynasty, woodblock printing replaced hand copying. In woodblock printing, a print is carved into a block of wood, which is then smeared with ink and used as a stamp. The Song also invented paper money, tea drinking, gunpowder, and the compass.

Unlike earlier dynasties, the Song dynasty invited regular people into the cities where markets and stores flourished. This city life spilled outside the walls where merchants and farmers built towns and sold things other than just food crops. People flocked to the cities from the surrounding countryside. Although people were chosen for government positions based on their skills, it was still the rich families who supplied most of the candidates for these positions.

The economy flourished under the Song dynasty as tea, silk, and ceramics were traded across the long Silk Road. This was a time of economic superiority and population growth.

Ming Dynasty: The Ming dynasty held power near the time of Columbus in the West, and like the Western civilizations of the time, the Ming were great explorers. From A.D. 1405–1433, Admiral Zheng led a flotilla of ships in exploration of the eastern coast of Africa. Under Admiral Zheng's command were 62 large ships and 255 smaller ships, which held a total of 27,000 people. This huge force brought gifts to the civilizations of Africa and the Middle East and asked for exotic gifts in return but did not try to extend the dynasty's territory.

The Great Wall of China was restored during the Ming dynasty.
Source: Corel

Civilizations of Asia *Reproducibles*

Government: Dynasties *(cont.)*

Ming Dynasty *(cont.)*: The Ming held examinations as a way to choose people for government jobs. These examinations were open to anybody, without regard to family background. The Ming also had a strong central government and a system of farms that made sure every person had enough food. The Ming dynasty is best remembered as a time of stability and exploration.

Questions: Write the answers to these questions here. Then, transfer them to the Information Wheel in the spot marked *Dynasties*.

1. List the three major medieval dynasties, and write a one-sentence description of each.

   _____
   _____
   _____
   _____
   _____
   _____

2. Define the word *dynasty*.

   _____
   _____

3. In these dynasties, how were government officials generally chosen?

   _____
   _____
   _____
   _____
   _____
   _____
   _____
   _____

©Shell Educational Publishing #9357 *Hands-on History: World History Activities*

Civilizations of Asia — *Reproducibles*

Government: Feudalism

Names: _____ Date: _____

Directions: Read the information on the next four pages and then complete the activities. When you have finished the activities, answer the questions and write these answers in the space on the Information Wheel marked *Feudalism*.

Have you ever heard the term *feud*? This word comes from the system of government called *feudalism*, in which many local governors fought each other for control of territory. In the Asian civilization you are studying, these local governors, called *daimyo*, owned land and allowed farmers to use the land as long as the farmers paid taxes. Many daimyo competed for power and would try to take over the lands of nearby estates. Because of this, each daimyo hired his own army of samurai to protect him, his land, and his farmers. For the samurai, the rules of honor, called *bushido*, stressed discipline, bravery, and simple living.

Activity

1. Read the descriptions of each class of people below.

2. Divide the classes of people among your group. Each group should illustrate and write a short description of one of the classes.

3. Get together with your group and try to put these classes in order, from highest to lowest in society.

Emperors: Emperors of this country were thought to hold a divine right to rule, meaning that they were chosen by God to be emperor. The current emperor of this country, named Akihito, is the 125th emperor, of which eight have been women.

Shoguns: At first, a shogun was appointed to be the supreme general of the army. Later, shoguns ruled the country and the emperor was little more than a figurehead, which means the emperor had little real power.

Civilizations of Asia　　　　　　　　　　　　　　　　　　　　　　　　　　　　　*Reproducibles*

Government: Feudalism (cont.)

Daimyos: A daimyo was a local governor who had control over a feudal estate. Often, daimyos fought each other for land. Though daimyos were allowed to do almost anything they pleased within their estates, they were supposed to be loyal to the central government.

Samurai: The samurai cared more about the rules of honor, called *bushido* than they did for their own lives or families. According to bushido, a samurai owed loyalty to his daimyo, to the shogun, and to the emperor. Samurai were highly educated and skilled in martial arts and horsemanship.

Ronin: Ronin are samurai who have no master. In this feudal society, ronin became farmers, monks, paid bodyguards, mercenaries (paid soldiers who would fight for anybody), or even robbers. Ronin were still bound by the rules of honor, called bushido.

Civilizations of Asia   *Reproducibles*

Government: Feudalism *(cont.)*

Peasants: Peasants farmed the land but did not own it. They were expected to pay taxes of up to two-thirds of their rice to their daimyo in return for protection during times of war. However, peasants were fairly well respected because they produced food. Peasants were by far the largest class, at 90 percent of the population.

Artisans: Artisans are very different from artists. Most artists were highly educated members of the upper class and could even be government officials; artisans were in charge of construction and building, and making functional things such as fishhooks, pots, and swords. Some artisans became well known for their skill, but as a whole, they were not respected because they didn't produce food.

Merchants: We think of merchants as well-off shop owners, but during the feudal period of this Asian society, they were thought to be less important than the people who created the goods they sold. This society thought that merchants lived off the work of others. Later, some merchants became so wealthy that they were able to hire ronin as their personal bodyguards.

Government: Feudalism (cont.)

Questions: Write the answers to these questions here. Then, transfer them to the Information Wheel in the spot marked *Feudalism*.

1. Which class did you choose as the lowest? Why?

   _____
   _____
   _____
   _____
   _____
   _____
   _____

2. Define the word *bushido*.

   _____
   _____

3. How does this society show its appreciation for nature?

   _____
   _____
   _____
   _____
   _____
   _____

4. Define the word *feudalism*.

   _____
   _____

Civilizations of Asia   Reproducibles

Mythology One

Names: _____   Date: _____

Directions: Read the information on this page and then complete the questions. When you have finished the questions, write the answers in the space on the Information Wheel marked *Mythology One*.

Flower Princess and Rock Princess

Ohkuninushi is the god or "Kami" of the land, and it is from Ohkuninushi that all emperors are descended. But Ohkuninushi didn't always live on the Earth; until his mother, the Sun Goddess, sent him to Earth to rule, he lived in the high plain of Heaven.

It was on his way from Heaven to Earth that the Kami met a girl named Konohanano-Sakuya-Hime, whose name means "princess blossoming brilliantly like the flowers of the trees." As you can guess by her name, this girl was very beautiful. In fact, she was so beautiful that Ohkuninushi proposed to her on the spot.

The father of the flower princess was very happy with the match, and wanted the couple to live forever in their happiness (happily ever after, of course), so along with the flower princess, he sent his other daughter to also be married to the Kami. Her name was Iwanaga-Hime, which means "princess as enduring as the rocks." Unfortunately, though the rock princess was enduring, she was not very pretty.

In fact, the rock princess was so not-very-pretty that Ohkuninushi turned her around and sent her back to her father on the spot.

The father was insulted and sent a message to the Kami. He said, "My reason for presenting my daughter, the flower princess, was so that the couple might live in beauty and prosperity; my reason for presenting my daughter, the rock princess, was so that the couple might also live eternally. By sending back the rock princess, the Kami and my daughter will live only as long as the blossoms on the trees."

And this is why emperors and the people of the world cannot live forever.

Questions: Write the answers to these questions on the Information Wheel in the spot marked *Mythology One*.

1. Which elements of nature can you find in this myth (list at least three)?
2. Does this culture believe that things are permanent or impermanent?
3. What values do you think this culture believes are important?

Civilizations of Asia   Reproducibles

Mythology Two

Names: _____   Date: _____

Directions: Read the information on this page and then complete the questions. When you have finished the questions, write the answers in the space on the Information Wheel marked *Mythology Two*.

The Story of Gajamugasuran

Once there was a ruler named Gajamugasuran who was granted great power by Lord Shiva. But this ruler didn't use his power kindly. He was very vain and forced his subjects to show their respect by doing *Thoeppukaranams*. Now, a Thoeppukaranam is an exercise and a kind of prayer where you cross your arms, hold your earlobes with opposite hands, and sit down and stand up. The ruler Gajamugasuran made his subjects do 1,008 Thoeppukaranams in the morning, 1,008 in the afternoon, and another 1,008 in the evening. Stop reading and try to do a Thoeppukaranam right now!

This ruler was like a demon gym teacher, and the people of the empire prayed to Lord Shiva to rescue them. Finally, Lord Shiva sent Ganesha, the remover of obstacles, to defeat the evil ruler. But back when Shiva and Gajamugasuran got along, Shiva had promised the ruler that he couldn't be killed by a weapon. So when Ganesha struck the evil ruler with his sword, bow and arrow, and ax, none of them had any effect.

Luckily, Ganesha had another plan—he broke off his tusk, which was not *technically* a weapon, and used it to stab Gajamugasuran. Instead of dying, the evil and vain ruler turned into a small mouse, which represented his vanity and ego, and continued to fight with Ganesha. Ganesha, the powerful elephant, sat on the mouse, crushing this representation of ego.

Questions: Write the answers to these questions on the Information Wheel in the spot marked *Mythology Two*.

1. What does Ganesha look like?

2. What is Ganesha's title (what does he do)?

3. What is the moral of this story (it has to do with vanity and ego)?

Civilizations of Asia   *Reproducibles*

Mythology Three

Names: _____ Date: _____

Directions: Read the information on the next three pages and then complete the questions. When you have finished the questions, write the answers in the space on the Information Wheel marked *Mythology Three*.

The Frog Who Became an Emperor

Once upon a time, there lived a very poor couple who were expecting a baby. Unfortunately, the father had to go away before the baby was born, but he made his wife promise to do all she could to raise the child. He said, "You and I are so poor that there is no hope for us now, but perhaps if our child is a boy, he will be able to earn his way out of poverty."

Three months after her husband's departure, the wife gave birth. The baby was neither a boy nor a girl, but a frog! The wife wept bitterly, but two months later, the frog-baby said his first words in a human voice. "Mother," he said, "my father is coming back tonight. I am going to wait for him beside the road." And sure enough, the husband did come home that very night.

"Where is my son?" the father asked as he walked in the door. "All I saw on the way home was a hideous frog sitting by the side of the road."

"That frog was your son," said the wife unhappily. The father looked heartbroken.

"But, how did my frog-son know I was coming home tonight?"

Just then the door opened and the frog-son came hopping in. "Because I know everything under heaven, father," the frog-son said.

The father and mother were amazed by his words and more amazed when he went on.

"Our country is in great peril," he said solemnly. "We are unable to resist the invaders. I want Father to take me to the emperor, for I must save our country."

The father was skeptical, but the frog-son persisted, and finally the father agreed to take his son to see the emperor. After a two day journey, they arrived at the capital, where they saw the written words of the emperor! "The imperial capital is in danger. My country has been invaded. We are willing to marry our daughter to the man who can drive away the enemy."

The frog-son tore down the decree and, with one gulp, swallowed it. The soldier guarding the emperor's words was greatly alarmed, but since the frog had swallowed the decree, he must be taken into the palace.

Civilizations of Asia   *Reproducibles*

Mythology Three (cont.)

The Frog Who Became an Emperor (cont.)

The emperor asked the frog if he knew how to defeat the enemy. The frog replied, "Yes, Lord." Then, the emperor asked him how many men and horses he would need.

"Not a single horse or a single man," answered the frog. "All I need is a heap of hot, glowing embers."

The emperor immediately commanded that a heap of hot, glowing embers be brought, and it was done. The heat was intense. The frog sat before the fire eating the flames by the mouthful for three days and three nights. He ate until his belly was as big and round as a bowling ball. By now the city was in great danger, for the enemy was already at the walls, but the frog behaved as if nothing unusual was happening and calmly went on swallowing fire and flame. Only after the third day had passed did he go to the top of the city wall and look at the situation. There, surrounding the city, were thousands of soldiers and horses, as far as the eye could see.

"Order your troops to put down their bows," said the frog, "and open the city gate."

The emperor turned pale with alarm when he heard these words. "What! With the enemy at our very door! You tell me to open the gate! How dare you trifle with me?"

"Your Imperial Highness has bidden me to drive the enemy away," said the frog. "And that is what I plan to do."

The emperor was helpless. He ordered the soldiers to stop bending their bows and lay down their arrows and throw open the gate.

As soon as the gate was open, the invaders poured in. The frog was above them in the gate tower, and as they passed underneath, he coolly and calmly spat fire down on them until the invaders fled in terror.

The emperor was overjoyed and the enemy was defeated! But the emperor still couldn't imagine having a frog as a son-in-law, and he went back on his word. "Let my daughter cast a ball into the crowd, and whoever catches it, she will wed!"

So the princess cast a ball from the castle wall, and it floated down toward the waiting people. As the crowd surged and reached for the ball, the frog drew in a mighty breath and, like a whirling tornado, sucked the ball straight to him.

Mythology Three *(cont.)*

The Frog Who Became an Emperor *(cont.)*

Now, surely, the princess will have to marry the frog! But the emperor was still unwilling to let this happen. "An embroidered ball cast by a princess," he declared, "can only be seized by a human hand. No beast may do so."

So the princess threw down a second ball, and it was caught by a handsome young man. Of course, this young man was the frog in disguise! The two were married, and by day the frog was a frog, but at night he stripped off his green skin and was transformed into the handsome young man.

Eventually, the emperor heard of this secret and asked the frog why he continued to wear the frog skin during the day. "Ah, Sire," replied the frog, "my frog skin is priceless. When I wear it in winter, I am warm and cozy, and in summer, cool and fresh. It is proof against wind and rain. Not even the fiercest flame can set it alight. And as long as I wear it, I can live for thousands of years."

Of course, the emperor demanded to try it on, and the frog, like a good subject, let him. But once the emperor had put on the frog skin, he was unable to take it off again! The frog put on the imperial robe and became the emperor. His father-in-law remained a frog forever.

Questions: Write the answers to these questions on the Information Wheel in the spot marked *Mythology Three*.

1. Does the poor couple think they can earn their way out of poverty, or are they content to be poor?

2. Does the frog have to come from a good family to join the government, or does he earn it through his intelligence?

3. Why is it just for the emperor to be punished? What did he do wrong?

4. Do you think this society respects women as equals? Why or why not?

Civilizations of Asia   *Reproducibles*

Civilizations of Asia Quiz

Name: _____ Date: _____

Directions: Circle the best answer to each question below.

1. Place the following terms in the correct spaces in the chart below: Feudalism, Empire, Dynasty, Shintoism, Hinduism/Islam, Confucianism, The Frog Who Became Emperor, Flower Princess and Rock Princess, The Story of Gajamugasuran.

	Government	**Religion**	**Myth**
India			
China			
Japan			

2. List two facts about each of the following religions or ways of thought.

   Shintoism: _____
   _____

   Confucianism: _____
   _____

   Hinduism: _____
   _____

   Islam: _____
   _____

3. List two facts about each of the following forms of government.

   Dynasty: _____
   _____

   Empire: _____
   _____

   Feudalism: _____
   _____

Habits of Mind Discussion

- How do religion, government, and myths relate to each other?

- Which of these Asian civilizations is most like ours? Why?

- What are the differences between Hinduism and Confucianism, thinking especially about possible movement between social classes?

- What are the differences among empire, dynasty, and feudalism as they were used in India, China, and Japan?

Europe in the Middle Ages   *Lesson Plans*

Europe in the Middle Ages

Overview

Students will work in small groups, each representing a feudal society, and will compete to be the first to build a castle. Groups will need to perform tasks that represent gathering the needed resources and expertise but will, at the same time, need to run their feudal cities. While the goal is to complete the castles, groups should not neglect the day-to-day workings of their societies, or they may (not) live to regret it.

The Tower of London, built during the Middle Ages
Source: Corbis

This game is fast-paced and fun, encouraging students to make quick decisions and act efficiently in order to beat other societies. As such, you will want to have a firm grasp of the rules before starting.

You will measure student learning through discussion, observation, and a reflection quiz. This activity also includes content-area writing assignments and primary source materials.

Objectives

- Students will understand how the culture of feudal society in Europe's Dark Ages influenced the scientific and technological choices of the time. (NCSS)
- Students will understand the structure of European feudal societies and will appreciate the difficulties they faced.

Materials

- copies of reproducibles (pages 118–140) as described on page 112
- textbooks, dictionaries, and other references for research
- 3 action-figure dolls (you can ask students to bring these)
- 5 manila envelopes
- 5 24" x 24" (61 cm x 61 cm) sheets of cardboard (for castle bases)
- extra (scrap) cardboard
- glue
- tape
- scissors
- pens and colored pencils

Europe in the Middle Ages   *Lesson Plans*

Europe in the Middle Ages *(cont.)*

Preparation

Total preparation time should be about 30 minutes each day, once all materials are gathered.

1. Make an information packet for each group containing a *Feudal Society Information* sheet (page 123), a *Task Menu* (page 124), a *Definitions* sheet (page 125), and cards totaling 500 pounds sterling from the *Pounds Sterling* sheet (page 122).
2. Organize a supplies table with the craft materials listed in the *Materials* section as well as five copies of each task (pages 126–137).
3. Copy and organize the following reference materials for your use during the game: *Activity Rules* sheet (pages 118–119), *Activity Flow Sheet* (page 121), *Easy Reference Chart* (page 120), the *Answer Key* (pages 115–117), and a cut-out copy of the *Time Will Tell Cards* (page 138), placed in a hat or box (to draw from).
4. Make a class set of the *Castle Quiz* (page 139).
5. Make an overhead of the *Habits of Mind Discussion* (page 140).

Directions

1. After reading the *Read-Aloud Directions* (pages 113–115), place the students in groups of four or five, and allow them to look over their information packets. They will be electing a lord and deciding on their first tasks. Warn students that when the activity starts, time could be a bit hectic, and there won't be a chance to ask questions. Allow time for students to ask any questions they may have.
2. You will want to make sure at least 30 minutes of class time remains before beginning the activity. Forty minutes would be ideal.
3. Allow ample time for cleanup at the end of the period.
4. Continue the activity the following day and perhaps into the day after.
5. After the game, refer to the *Habits of Mind Discussion* for guided discussion.
6. After the discussion, pass out the *Castle Quiz*. Students can complete this at home, if pressed for time.

Things to Consider

1. Groups will need to elect a responsible and organized lord, who will make intelligent decisions. Emphasize the importance of this character in order to avoid a simple popularity contest when groups vote for their leaders.
2. This game seems complex, though with strong lords it will run smoothly. Make sure that you take time beforehand to understand the rules of the game. Once the activity starts, there will be little time for reassessment. The groups compete against each other and against the clock and generally don't take kindly to changes in the rules as the game progresses.

Europe in the Middle Ages (cont.)

Things to Consider (cont.)

3. Groups may sacrifice craftsmanship in favor of speed, creating a shoddy final product. Don't mark tasks as finished until students have completed them with satisfactory results. You might also let students know that you will be displaying their castles at the end of the activity.
4. If groups are off-task or unnecessarily loud at any point in the activity, fine them in pounds sterling.
5. Money management will be a major issue for most groups; encourage students, and especially lords, to come up with a strategy before the start of the game. If paper money proves too cumbersome for you, consider doing away with it entirely and keeping track of groups' money on an overhead projector.

Read-Aloud Directions

People who lived in Europe in the Middle Ages lived according to the feudal system. In the feudal system, one lord owned all the land in an area and peasants, called vassals, could farm this land as long as they paid taxes. Sometimes taxes were so high that farmers worked more like slaves. But the lord and his knights had another important duty—they were responsible for protecting their vassals in case of attack. In the early Middle Ages, lords battled each other for power and each lord controlled what was almost a city-state. *[Ask students to define the word* city-state.*]*

During the later Middle Ages, all the lords in a country were united under a common king, but with England and France at war with each other, the vassals still needed protection. When one country attacked the other, all the attacked people would rush inside the walls of their great castle, where they would be safe.

Castles started out as wooden forts with walls of pointy logs, but as attackers learned to overrun wooden castles, they developed into huge rock goliaths. Not only did castles have 50-foot (15 m) tall walls that were upwards of 10 feet (0.3 m) thick, but they were also full of technology and tricks meant to keep attackers out and the people safe inside. For example, many castles had only one way in or out which was called the gatehouse. A gatehouse might have a drawbridge over a deep moat that the lord could raise up, leaving a gap that attackers had to cross. Once attackers were across the moat, things didn't get any easier—from atop the gatehouse, the lord and his knights could pour boiling oil. Lining the walls of the gatehouse, there might be arrow slits where defenders could shoot at attackers while staying

Europe in the Middle Ages (cont.)

Read-Aloud Directions (cont.)

protected themselves. Sometimes the only thing attackers could do was to lay siege to the castle—they would camp outside the walls until the lord and his people ran out of food.

Castles were used for protection and were also used to show a lord's strength. If the farmers were to stay happy while working like slaves, they had to know they would be protected by a strong lord.

For the next couple of days, you are going to work in small groups, with each group becoming a feudal society. Societies will be competing to build castles. You will need to gather all your resources and expertise before you can start building. But while you are gathering resources, don't forget to run your feudal society. If you neglect the daily tasks of your kingdom, you might regret it later.

This game sounds a bit complex at first, but there are packets of information that I will hand out later that will lead you through it pretty easily. That being said, it's still important for everybody to hear all the complex directions so you can't accuse me of changing the rules later. Please hold your questions until I've read all the rules.

1. Your goal is to build a castle.

2. You will be working in small groups, trying to complete the four construction tasks needed to build a castle. While you are working on construction tasks, you will also have to keep your feudal society running by completing kingdom tasks. Remember, you only need construction tasks to build your castle, but if you neglect kingdom tasks, you may regret it later.

3. Both construction tasks and kingdom tasks cost pounds sterling. You will start with 500 pounds sterling and will need to pay me 300 pounds for each construction task and 150 bags for each kingdom task. You can also earn pounds sterling by filling out your Definitions sheet.

4. Each group will elect a lord who will be in charge of keeping track of your pounds sterling and who will choose which construction and kingdom tasks to buy.

5. The game is split into years and roundtables. Each year is 10-minutes long. During years, groups work on the two types of tasks while the group's lord decides which tasks to buy next. In the roundtables (between years), each group gets another 500 pounds sterling, which the lords will use to buy tasks for the next year.

Europe in the Middle Ages (cont.)

Read-Aloud Directions (cont.)

6. Also during roundtables, I will draw one of the Time Will Tell Cards. These cards contain random events, both negative and positive, that might affect your empire. Guard against the negative effects of the cards by completing kingdom tasks.

7. If a member of your feudal society dies due to a Time Will Tell Card, he or she will have to fill out a Birth Certificate sheet in order to rejoin the game. Every person in your group must die once before you can repeat.

8. There are two stages to each task, which I will mark on a special sheet. When you buy the task, you get a W, meaning you are working on it. When you finish the task, you will get an F. If you do not complete a task in the same year you bought it, you will need to pay for it again to keep working on it, so don't buy more tasks than you can complete in a year! If at any point in the game you can't pay pounds sterling for something, one member of your feudal society will die (and will need to complete a Birth Certificate before rejoining the game).

9. Remember, the lord chooses tasks and manages your pounds sterling; the rest of the group works on tasks. Complete the five construction tasks, but don't forget kingdom tasks or you might get hurt by Time Will Tell Cards.

10. This is a lot of information to remember! Don't worry, all the directions are in your information packets. *[Put students in groups, give them five minutes to explore their packets, elect a lord, and begin.]*

Answer Key

Definitions (page 125): Give 50 pounds sterling for each correct definition.

1. Siege: When an army camps outside castle walls, hoping to starve out the defenders
2. Chivalry: The medieval code of honor, especially courtesy toward women
3. Coat of Arms: A design that signifies a particular family or city
4. Feudalism: The legal and social system of medieval Europe
5. Vassal: A farmer/peasant subject who paid taxes in exchange for protection
6. Crusade: A military expedition made by Christians against Muslim forces in the holy land
7. Moat: A wide ditch dug around castles for protection, usually filled with water
8. Charlemagne: An important king in medieval Europe
9. Serf: A medieval slave who worked the land and was bought and sold with it
10. Manor: A fine house and the land surrounding it

Europe in the Middle Ages (cont.)

Answer Key (cont.)

Birth Certificate I (page 126)

Birth Certificate II (page 127)
Students should write at least five lines describing their ultimate walled city.

Birth Certificate III (page 128)
1. feudalism
2. Gaul
3. chain mail
4. drawbridge

Final Answer: Charlemagne

Castle Plans (page 129)
Students will use poster paper and pens to draw plans for their castles including the following elements: kitchens, great halls, spiral staircases, gatehouses, chapel, bedrooms, and courtyards. These plans need to be clean and usable enough so that students can follow them when creating their castles at the end of this activity.

Gatehouse (page 130)
Students will use craft supplies to create gatehouses, including the following parts: drawbridges and portcullises guarding arched tunnel entrances, crenellations (the squares across the top), towers on either side of the entrances, and small windows.

Chapel (page 131)
Students will color in the stained glass windows and write at least four sentences describing what they think is going on in the scene in the window.

Europe in the Middle Ages (cont.)

Answer Key (cont.)

Moat Monster (page 132)

Each group will draw a moat monster and write an ode to it. The ode should be at least four lines long and should contain the monster's name and description.

Farming (page 133)

Students should fill in the chart with the following jobs:

Month	Job	Weather
January	Mending and making tools and repairing fences	Showers
April	Spring sowing of seeds and harrowing	Showers and sunshine
August	Harvesting	Warm, dry
November	Collecting fallen acorns for pigs	Showers and sunshine

Students should also write the following short definitions:
1. marl: soil containing clay and limestone, often with shell and other minerals
2. fallow: a field left unseeded and unplowed
3. harrow: a piece of farm equipment used to break up dirt clods
4. sow: to plant seeds
5. thresh: to separate seeds from straw, chaff, and husks

Blacksmith (page 134)

Each group will bring you an action figure completely covered in decorated paper armor (except for the bottom of the figure's feet so that it can still stand). Manipulate the action figure; if the armor rips, students will need to try again.

Games (page 135)

Students will create a game board and pieces for the Viking game "Hnefetafl." One member of the task society will play one member from any other society. If the task society wins, the task is complete. If the opposing society wins, the task society must pay the opposing society 250 pounds sterling (if they cannot pay, one society member dies), and the task society must find another person to play again.

Doctors (page 136)

Students should create a neat poster illustrating the four humors (black bile, yellow bile, phlegm, and blood), and should make up, write, and illustrate fanciful cures for leprosy, plague, fever, and dysentery.

Castle Quiz (page 139)

1. B
2. D
3. B
4. A
5. D
6. C
7. A
8. C
9. B

Europe in the Middle Ages *Reproducibles*

Activity Rules

1. Students work in five groups (4–6 students per group) representing feudal societies and compete to build castles.

2. To build a castle, each group must do the following three things:
   - Complete the four construction tasks
   - Keep at least one member alive at any given time
   - Complete the *Definitions* sheet

3. Each group will elect a lord who will be in charge of choosing tasks and managing the group's money (pounds sterling).

4. Before beginning each year of the game (represented by 10 minutes of class time), each lord will decide what to purchase from the *Task Menu* (page 124). The lord will buy construction tasks for 300 pounds sterling each, or kingdom tasks for 150 pounds each. When groups buy tasks, you should mark a *W* for "working" on the *Activity Flow Sheet* next to each task in the year purchased.

5. Then, start a 10-minute timer. At the organized supplies table, groups will find the sheet that describes the task(s) they purchased and will have the remainder of the 10 minutes for work on tasks, while the lord decides how pounds sterling will be spent during the next roundtable.

6. At the end of 10 minutes, stop time to assess the year and prepare for the next. This time is known as a roundtable and should take no more than three minutes.

7. During the roundtable, quickly assess each project and mark either *F* for finished or another *W* if a group needs to continue to work. Also, if a group does not finish a task in the year they purchased it, they will need to pay for the task again. This creates time pressure to finish the tasks and will help keep students on task.

Europe in the Middle Ages   *Reproducibles*

Activity Rules *(cont.)*

8. Also during the roundtable, draw a *Time Will Tell Card*, read it to the class, and follow through with the effects described on the card. If a group cannot pay, one member will die. If a member dies for any reason, he or she will need to complete a *Birth Certificate* sheet in order to rejoin the game.

9. Another 500 pounds sterling will be distributed to each lord for use in the coming year. Additionally, students may earn 50 pounds per finished definition on the *Definitions* sheet, to be distributed at any point. The lords will purchase tasks, and the next year will commence.

10. The game continues with lords purchasing tasks and managing pounds sterling and the remaining students completing the tasks. When a group completes the four construction tasks, give the group a *Castle Construction* sheet (page 137).

11. The first group to complete the castle wins, though you should not explicitly tell students this at the game's outset to avoid groups losing motivation if they get irredeemably behind.

For a concise description of the parts of the game, see the *Easy Reference Chart* (page 120).

Europe in the Middle Ages   *Reproducibles*

Easy Reference Chart

Years (groups work on tasks)	**Roundtables** (groups stop working)
While groups work, each lord decides how the pounds sterling will be spent during the next roundtable.	• Give each group 500 pounds sterling. • Teacher draws, reads, and collects on a *Time Will Tell Card*. • Lords purchase construction tasks for 300 pounds and daily tasks for 150 pounds. • Teacher marks *W* or *F* on the *Activity Flow Sheet*

Don't forget that groups will be penalized pounds sterling for any off-task behavior. At the end of the day, gather all pounds sterling and excess materials, and put them in the group envelope.

Europe in the Middle Ages   *Reproducibles*

Activity Flow Sheet

			Year 1	Year 2	3	4	5	6	7	8
Group 1 Lord:	Const.	Castle Plans								
		Gatehouse								
		Chapel								
		Moat Monster								
	Kingdom	Farming								
		Blacksmiths								
		Games								
		Doctors								
Group 2 Lord:	Const.	Castle Plans								
		Gatehouse								
		Chapel								
		Moat Monster								
	Kingdom	Farming								
		Blacksmiths								
		Games								
		Doctors								
Group 3 Lord:	Const.	Castle Plans								
		Gatehouse								
		Chapel								
		Moat Monster								
	Kingdom	Farming								
		Blacksmiths								
		Games								
		Doctors								
Group 4 Lord:	Const.	Castle Plans								
		Gatehouse								
		Chapel								
		Moat Monster								
	Kingdom	Farming								
		Blacksmiths								
		Games								
		Doctors								
Group 5 Lord:	Const.	Castle Plans								
		Gatehouse								
		Chapel								
		Moat Monster								
	Kingdom	Farming								
		Blacksmiths								
		Games								
		Doctors								

Europe in the Middle Ages   *Reproducibles*

Pounds Sterling

Europe in the Middle Ages *Reproducibles*

Feudal Society Information

Names: _____ Date: _____

Directions: The first thing you need to do is elect a lord. Your lord will be responsible for managing your pounds sterling and picking which construction and kingdom tasks your society will work on (with some of the group's input). Go ahead—elect a lord!

Okay, now that you have a lord, you're ready to rule your feudal society. Here's what to do:

- In a couple of minutes the game will start. Use this time to decide how you will spend your first 500 pounds sterling (look at the *Task Menu*). Each year, you will get another 500 pounds. At any point, you can earn more pounds by filling out your *Definitions* sheet.

- Remember, your lord's job is to decide which tasks your group will purchase during the roundtables between years. The group's job is to complete the tasks quickly. (If you don't finish in a year, you have to pay for it again, so don't buy more tasks than you can complete in a year!)

- Your goal is to finish the four construction tasks and then to build a castle, but you might need to complete some kingdom tasks, or you will regret it when the teacher draws a *Time Will Tell Card*.

- If a situation ever arises when you can't pay what's required, one group member will die.

- If someone dies, he or she must fill out a *Birth Certificate* sheet before rejoining the game. Every person must die once before you can repeat.

Europe in the Middle Ages   *Reproducibles*

Task Menu

Names: _____   Date: _____

Construction Tasks (300 pounds sterling each)

Castle Plans
You can't build a castle without plans! You will need to work together to make sure your plans include all the needed parts.

Gatehouse
The gatehouse is the entryway to your castle—you want friends to be able to get in, but you also want to keep enemies out. Building a gatehouse will be your most complex task.

Chapel
Religion was very important to Europeans in the Middle Ages. Without a chapel, no castle would be complete.

Moat Monster
What good is a moat without a moat monster? You will need to create your own monster, and write an ode to your creature.

Kingdom Tasks (150 pounds sterling each)

Farming
Farmers need to grow enough food for themselves and also need to pay taxes on their land.

Blacksmiths
Blacksmiths created all the metal objects a feudal society needed, including horseshoes, ploughs, swords, and armor.

Games
Peasants played games in any spare time they had to alleviate their boredom.

Doctors
Guard against the ravages of disease by training doctors for your feudal society.

Don't forget to complete your *Definitions* sheet!

Europe in the Middle Ages   *Reproducibles*

Definitions

Names: _____ Date: _____

Directions: Write definitions for the terms on this sheet to earn more money. You may need to look for answers in your textbook, dictionaries, or encyclopedias. When you finish, show this sheet to your teacher. For every correct answer, you can earn an additional 50 pounds sterling.

1. siege

   _____

2. chivalry

   _____

3. coat of arms

   _____

4. feudalism

   _____

5. vassal

   _____

6. crusade

   _____

7. moat

   _____

8. Charlemagne

   _____

9. serf

   _____

10. manor

    _____

Europe in the Middle Ages *Reproducibles*

Birth Certificate I

Name: _____ Date: _____

You're dead! Complete this sheet to rejoin the game. Show your teacher when you're done.

Directions: Place at least five of the following country names on the correct places in the map below. You might need to use your textbook, an atlas, or an encyclopedia. Remember, these were the countries of the Middle Ages, and they look a little different than they do today.

- France
- Holy Roman Empire
- England
- Scotland
- Kingdom of Norway
- Kingdom of Sweden
- Kingdom of Denmark
- Kingdom of Poland
- Kingdom of Hungary
- Russia

Europe in the Middle Ages *Reproducibles*

Birth Certificate II

Name: _____   Date:

You're dead! Complete this sheet to rejoin the game. Show your teacher when you're done.

Directions: Write a description of your ultimate walled city. What would you include inside? How would you defend it? Make sure your description takes up at least five lines, using regular-size writing.

_____
_____
_____
_____
_____
_____
_____
_____
_____
_____
_____
_____
_____
_____
_____
_____
_____
_____
_____
_____

Europe in the Middle Ages   *Reproducibles*

Birth Certificate III

Name: _____ Date: _____

You're dead! Complete this sheet to rejoin the game. Show your teacher when you're done.

Directions: Answer the questions below to decode the message and discover the name of the first great ruler of the Middle Ages.

1. What was the basis of government in the Middle Ages called?

   $\underline{\text{F}} \ \underline{} \ \underline{} \ \underline{} \ \underline{} \ \underline{} \ \underline{} \ \underline{\text{M}}$
      1   2   3   4

2. In the Middle Ages, present-day France was known as

   $\underline{} \ \underline{} \ \underline{\text{U}} \ \underline{\text{L}}$
     5   6

3. The layer of armor made up of interlocking steel rings was called

   $\underline{} \ \underline{} \ \underline{\text{A}} \ \underline{\text{I}} \ \underline{} \ \underline{} \ \underline{\text{A}} \ \underline{\text{I}} \ \underline{}$
     7   8   9

4. One of the elements of a castle's defense system

   $\underline{} \ \underline{} \ \underline{} \ \underline{\text{W}} \ \underline{} \ \underline{} \ \underline{} \ \underline{} \ \underline{} \ \underline{}$
         10   11

Write each letter from the clues in the box above the correct number.

7	8	2	10	3	1	4	6	5	9	11

Europe in the Middle Ages   Reproducibles

Castle Plans

Names: _____   Date: _____

Directions: On poster paper, draw a plan of your castle like the one shown below. You will need to draw both the ground and the first floor, and you will need to include the following things: kitchen, great hall, spiral staircases, gatehouse (shown at the bottom of these plans), chapel, bedrooms, and courtyard. Take your time to do a good job, because you will be following this plan when you build your castle. If your group has already built its gatehouse, be sure to draw it correctly on these plans

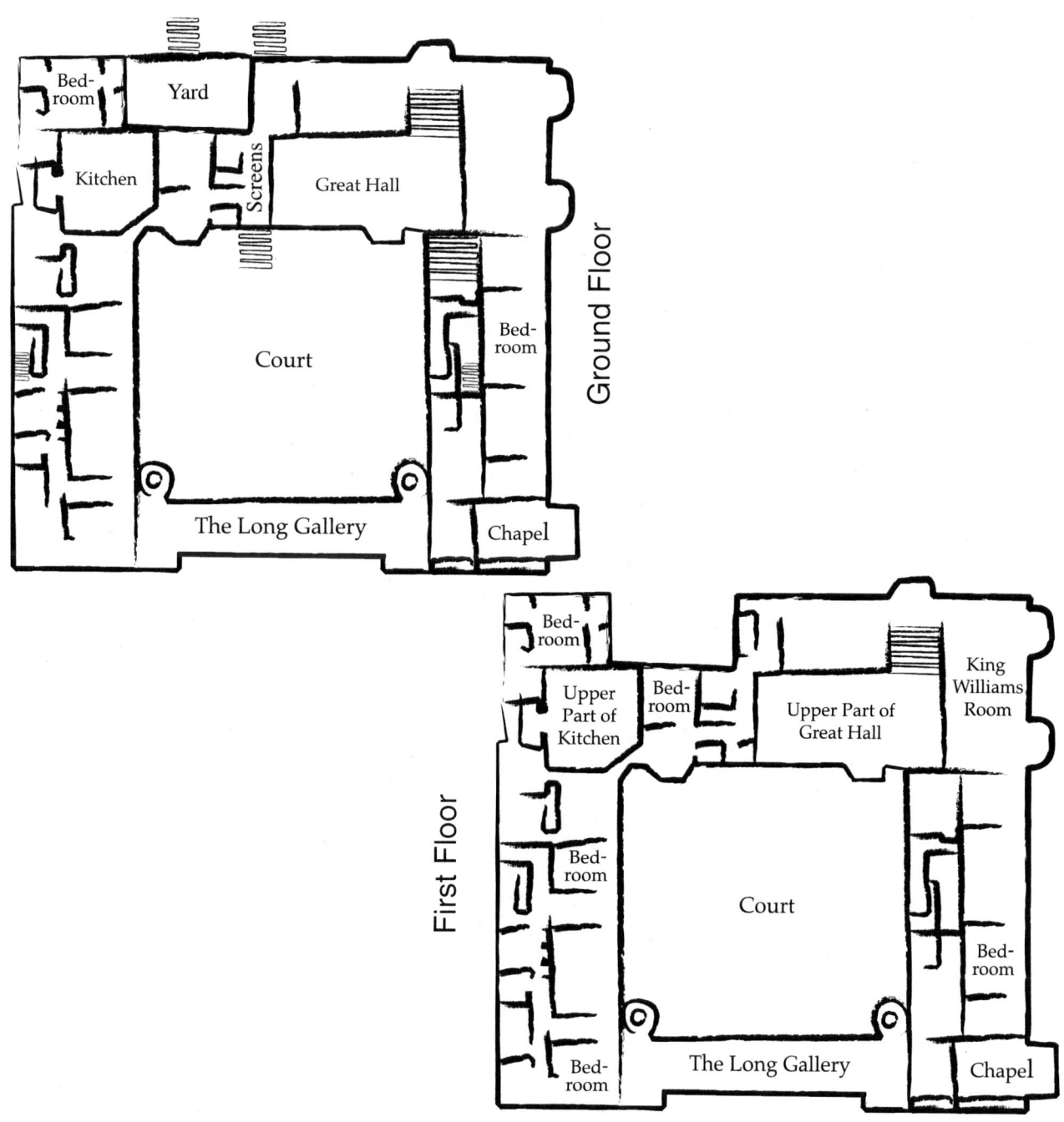

©Shell Educational Publishing   129   #9357 Hands-on History: World History Activities

Europe in the Middle Ages *Reproducibles*

Gatehouse

Names: _____ Date: _____

Unfortunately for a castle's lord, it was necessary to leave a gap in the thick walls for people to get in and out. This gap in the wall was guarded by a gatehouse, the most important piece of a castle's defense.

Directions: Look at the picture below. Use any craft supplies you choose and your *Castle Plans* sheet (if complete) to create the gatehouse for your castle. Your gatehouse needs to have the following parts: drawbridge and portcullis guarding an arched tunnel entrance, crenellations (the squares across the top), towers on either side of the entrance, and small windows.

Europe in the Middle Ages   *Reproducibles*

Chapel

Names: _____   Date: _____

Religion was very important to the people of medieval Europe. For example, one of the ways that kings controlled all the lords in their countries was by controlling the church. If a lord got out of line, the church could threaten to "excommunicate" him, meaning the lord would be kicked out of the church. If you were excommunicated, nobody would have anything to do with you. So by controlling the church, a king could make sure each of the lords did what he wanted.

Many medieval chapels had stained-glass windows. These windows depicted scenes and stories from the Christian religion or from history. These windows acted as a picture Bible for the many people who couldn't read.

Directions: Color the stained-glass window below, and on the back of this page, write at least four sentences describing what you think is going on in the scene in this window.

Europe in the Middle Ages   *Reproducibles*

Moat Monster

Names: _____   Date: _____

Many castles were supposedly guarded not only by human defenders, but also by a monster that lived deep in the castle's moat.

Directions: Create your own moat monster in the space below. Draw your monster, name it, and then label the special features of your monster that make it especially fearsome. When you are done creating your monster, you will write an ode describing it on a separate piece of paper. An ode is a lyric poem written in rhyme. Yours needs to be at least four lines long and needs to contain your monster's name and description.

Europe in the Middle Ages   *Reproducibles*

Farming

Names: _____ Date: _____

If you were a peasant in medieval Europe, you followed something called the farming year. In every month, there were specific jobs you had to do and a certain type of weather that would be best for your crops.

Directions: Place the following jobs in the correct blank months in the chart below after thinking about the order you would have to do things. One month will have two jobs: mending and making tools; repairing fences; harvesting; spring sowing of seeds and harrowing; and collecting fallen acorns for pigs.

Month	Job	Weather
January		showers
February	carting manure and marl	showers
March	ploughing and spreading of fallow fields	dry, no severe frosts
April		showers and sunshine
May	digging ditches, first ploughing of fallow fields	showers and sunshine
June	haymaking, second ploughing of fallow field, sheep-shearing	dry
July	haymaking, sheep-shearing, weeding of crops	dry early, showers later
August		warm and dry
September	threshing, ploughing and pruning fruit trees	showers
October	last ploughing of the year	dry, no severe frosts
November		showers and sunshine
December	mending and making tools, killing animals	showers and sunshine

Next, on the back of this sheet, define the following terms (you may need to look them up in your textbook or in a dictionary).

1. marl
2. fallow
3. harrow
4. sow
5. thresh

©Shell Educational Publishing

Europe in the Middle Ages   *Reproducibles*

Blacksmiths

Names: _____ Date: _____

Blacksmiths were in charge of making everything metal, including horseshoes, swords, and ploughs. But the most complex job of the blacksmith was to create armor. Medieval societies even had a special kind of blacksmith, called an armorer, whose job it was just to make armor for princes and kings.

Working over hot coals, armorers would heat up sheets of metal and then pound them into shape. Once all the pieces were shaped, armorers welded them together to create fine suits that were light and flexible but could withstand even a heavy sword.

Directions: Use paper and tape to make a flexible suit of armor for one of the action figures on the crafts table. Every part of the action figure needs to be covered except for the bottoms of its feet, and the action figure needs to keep its full range of movement. Make sure you decorate your armor using pens and/or paints. When you are finished, your teacher will wiggle the arms and legs; if your armor rips, you will need to try again.

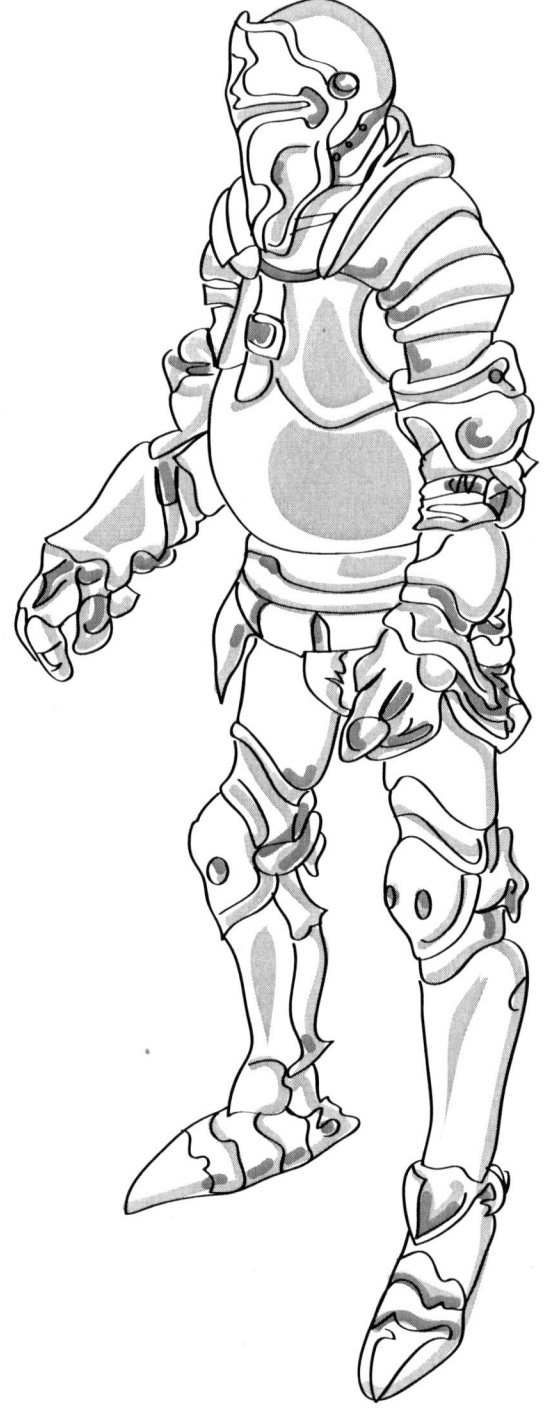

Europe in the Middle Ages — *Reproducibles*

Games

Names: _____   Date: _____

While peasant life in medieval Europe was difficult, it wasn't completely boring. Sometimes peasants could find a spare minute to play games, and one of their favorites was called *Hnefatafl*, which was a Viking game much like chess.

Directions: On posterboard, draw a 7 x 7 grid with squares as large as the paper will allow. This will be your game board. Next, create 8 white markers, 16 black markers, and a marker for the king. Put the markers on the board as shown below. You now need to pick one member of your society and find a member of a *different* society who will play against you. If you win, the task is complete. If your opponent wins, you will need to pay his or her society 250 pounds sterling (and if you can't pay, one of your society members will die). This is a high-stakes game! Also, you will probably not complete this in one year, so get ready to pay another 150 pounds sterling.

Hnefatafl Rules

1. Set up the game board as shown to the right.

2. The goal for the person playing white is to move the king to one of the corners of the board. The goal for the black player is to trap the king.

3. Each turn, you may move any one piece in a straight line, either up and down or side to side but not diagonally (like a rook in chess). You may not jump over pieces.

4. If you sandwich your opponent's piece between two of your pieces (either up and down or side to side), you trap your opponent's piece and can take it off the board. You can take many pieces at once. You can trap your opponent against the corner square with only one piece.

5. It takes four black pieces to trap the king, unless the king is against a side or against the corner.

White moves first. Go ahead, play *Hnefatafl*!

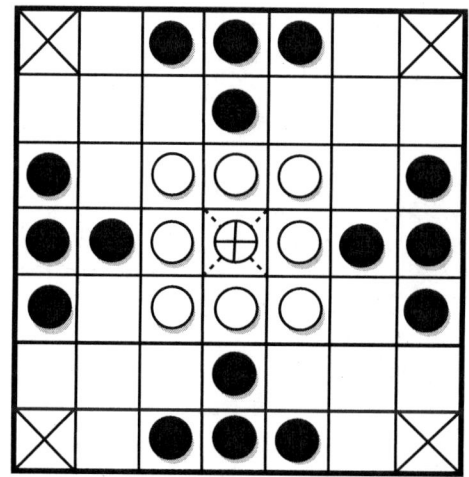

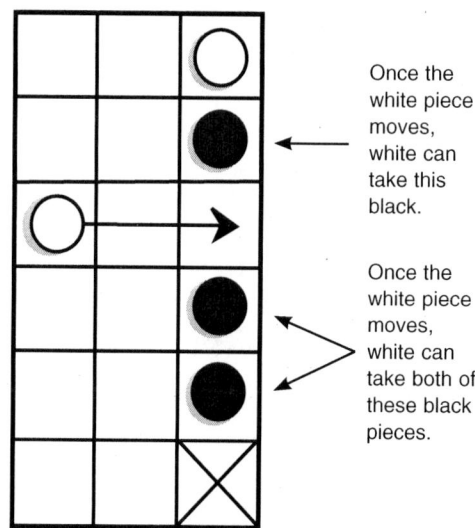

Once the white piece moves, white can take this black.

Once the white piece moves, white can take both of these black pieces.

Europe in the Middle Ages   *Reproducibles*

Doctors

Names: _____ Date: _____

Medieval doctors believed that inside the body there were four humors. If these humors got out of balance, it would cause sickness. Each humor was either hot or cold, dry or moist, and was associated with one of the elements (fire, earth, air, water). The goal of medieval medicine was to balance these humors, which doctors generally did by letting the unbalanced humor out of the body. For example, if a person had a "sanguine temperament," doctors might use leeches to draw out the person's extra blood. Doctors believed bloodletting was especially effective if they said the Lord's Prayer while operating. The four humors and their qualities are shown in the chart below.

The Four Humors and Their Qualities		
	Hot	**Cold**
Dry	Yellow Bile, Choleric Temperament, Fire	Black Bile, Melancholic Temperament, Earth
Moist	Blood, Sanguine Temperament, Air	Phlegm, Phlegmatic Temperament, Water

Directions: On poster paper, enlarge the chart above and illustrate each of the four humors. Then, make up, write, and illustrate ways that medieval doctors might have treated the following common illnesses. If you don't know what the illness is, look it up in your textbook or in a dictionary. Be creative!

- leprosy
- plague
- fever
- dysentery

Europe in the Middle Ages   *Reproducibles*

Castle Construction

Names: _____ Date: _____

Congratulations! You have completed the four construction tasks! Now all you have to do is create your castle. However, if you choose, you can still have some of your group members work on kingdom tasks so that you don't get hurt by *Time Will Tell Cards* while you work on the castle.

Directions

1. Get a sheet of cardboard to use as the base of your castle.

2. On this cardboard base, draw the castle plans you already completed.

3. Use any craft supplies you choose to build your castle. One good way to do this is to cut long strips of cardboard and then cut chunks off this strip to make your walls—this way all your walls will be the same height.

4. Don't forget to include the gatehouse you already built!

5. Decorate your castle using pens or colored pencils. You might want to draw a moat and a picture of your moat monster.

Europe in the Middle Ages   *Reproducibles*

Time Will Tell Cards

Time Will Tell
A middle class of merchants and bankers is starting to develop in your feudal society. More people also means you need more food to feed them. If you haven't completed farming, you must pay 300 pounds sterling to buy food from your neighbors.

Time Will Tell
Half your food stores are infested with weevils! It's a good thing you focused on farming and have enough to spare. Uh oh! If you haven't completed farming, one member of your group dies of starvation.

Time Will Tell
Metal tools made everything easier, from farming to fighting to chopping wood. If you haven't yet hired a town blacksmith, you are not as productive as you could be—pay 250 pounds sterling.

Time Will Tell
Your lord is sick! If you don't have a doctor, you need to pay 400 pounds sterling to hire a doctor from a neighboring society. If you can't pay, your lord dies!

Time Will Tell
You are attacked by Visigoths from the north! While you sustain losses, it's a good thing you are under the protection of a strong lord or you would be wiped out completely. If you have hired a blacksmith, you can fight with metal tools and only one member of your group dies. If you have no blacksmith, two people in your group die.

Time Will Tell
Have you completed *Games*? If not, play rock-paper-scissors to choose one of the members of your society. This person moves somewhere more fun (even if it's the lord) and joins another group of the teacher's choice.

Time Will Tell
If you haven't completed *Games*, life in your society is too boring. Pay 250 pounds sterling to hire traveling troubadours to entertain your people.

Time Will Tell
The black plague sweeps through Europe! If you have a doctor, only one member of your group dies. If you don't have a doctor, two members of your group die.

Europe in the Middle Ages   *Reproducibles*

Castle Quiz

Name: _____ Date: _____

Directions: Circle the best answer to each question below.

1. What was the medieval system of social organization called?
   - A. democracy
   - B. feudalism
   - C. republic
   - D. theocracy

2. Which one of the following is least like the others?
   - A. serf
   - B. peasant
   - C. vassal
   - D. lord

3. Which of the following is **NOT** a common castle defense?
   - A. moat
   - B. feudalism
   - C. gatehouse
   - D. crenellations

4. A metal gate that drops straight down out of a gatehouse was known as a
   - A. portcullis.
   - B. barrier.
   - C. porterhouse.
   - D. shield.

5. Which of the following was an important medieval king?
   - A. Julius Caesar
   - B. Alexander the Great
   - C. Catherine the Great
   - D. Charlemagne

6. Medieval doctors believed that an imbalance of these substances caused sicknesses.
   - A. the four horsemen
   - B. the four tops
   - C. the four humors
   - D. the four winds

7. Which of the following describes the social order of medieval Europe from lowest to highest class?
   - A. serf, vassal, lord, king
   - B. serf, lord, vassal, king
   - C. vassal, serf, lord, king
   - D. vassal, lord, serf, king

8. Peasants farmed the land and paid ____ in exchange for ____.
   - A. pounds sterling; food
   - B. taxes; the right to vote
   - C. taxes; protection
   - D. labor; horses

9. If a lord disobeyed the church, he might be
   - A. disavowed.
   - B. excommunicated.
   - C. disowned.
   - D. crucified.

Europe in the Middle Ages — *Reproducibles*

Habits of Mind Discussion

- Describe two things you learned through each task.

- Why did lords need vassals? Why did vassals need lords? Was this a fair trade?

- How is the feudal system similar to other forms of government you know?

- What were the purposes of a castle?

- Would you have wanted to live in medieval Europe? Why or why not?

Renaissance and Reformation   *Lesson Plans*

Renaissance and Reformation

Overview

Working in small groups, students will role-play museum curators who are trying to match listed artifacts with the correct Renaissance country of origin. As information about each country's culture is provided in stages, students will revise their views of history based on changing information. After recreating works of art using the techniques of the chosen artworks, each group will present its country to the class and will place all the created artworks in its country's display in your classroom Renaissance Museum.

Students will gain an overview of Renaissance history and culture and will explore the difficulties in piecing together the past from incomplete information. As many of their initial artwork/country pairings will be wrong, students will learn the changing nature of history and the need for historical revision as new information comes to light. This activity uses primary source materials and incorporates art activities. Student learning will be measured through discussion, evaluation of activity sheets, and a short quiz.

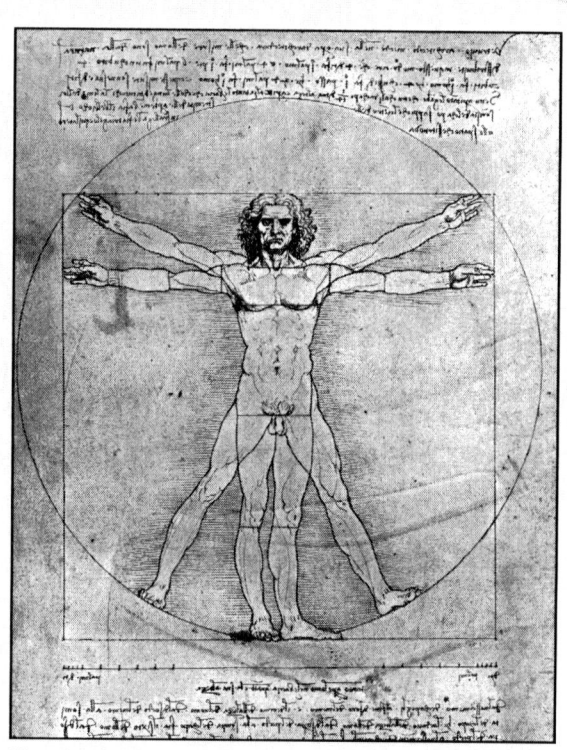

Sketch of the human anatomy by Leonardo Da Vinci
Source: Clipart.com

Objectives

- Students will understand that modern scholars may describe the same event in different ways but must provide reasons and evidence for their views. (NCSS)
- Students will gain an overview of the rebirth of culture and classical ideals in Renaissance Europe.

Materials

- copies of reproducibles (pages 145–175) as described on page 142
- poster paper
- pens
- colored pencils
- paints (optional)

Renaissance and Reformation (cont.)

Preparation

Total preparation time should be about 30 minutes.

Day One

Make copies of the following reproducibles.

- *Renaissance Country* activity sheets (pages 145–152); so that each student gets a copy of his or her country's sheet
- *Artworks Master Sheet* (pages 153–154), one per group
- *Curator Tasks* sheet (page 155), one per group
- Artwork task sheets (pages 156–167), one copy of each per student

Set up a craft table with all the materials listed on page 141.

Day Two

Make sure that art materials from day one are still available.

Make one copy per group of each of the *History* sheets (pages 168–172).

Day Three

Set up an area of the room (the museum) where you can display student artifacts. All art can be hung on the walls. Label the museum with space for each of the four time periods.

Copy the *Habits of Mind Discussion* (page 175) onto an overhead or write the information on the board. Make a classroom set of the *Renaissance Art Quiz* (pages 173–174).

Directions

Day One

1. After reading the *Read-Aloud Directions* (page 144), split students into four groups of curators, each working on a different country (Italy, the Netherlands, France, and Germany). Group students into designated areas of the room, where they will first read and individually complete a *Renaissance Country* activity sheet.
2. Once students complete the sheets, allow them group discussion time to rank and circle five items on the *Artworks Master Sheet*. The directions are included on the sheet.
3. The class will now choose their artworks. To avoid duplication, go around the class with each country, choosing one artwork per turn until all artworks have been chosen (three rounds). On the board, write the country and the three artworks the students choose.
4. Distribute the artwork task sheets, and allow groups time to look them over. If there are any paintings that groups no longer think are from their country, they may trade them with another group.
5. When groups have solidified their picks, ask them to complete the *Curator Tasks* sheet, assigning each student to work on specific artworks.
6. Once students show you their *Curator Tasks* sheet, they will spend the remainder of the period (and perhaps longer if needed) creating artworks using the artwork task sheets.

Renaissance and Reformation — Lesson Plans

Renaissance and Reformation (cont.)

Directions (cont.)

Day Two

1. Students will spend the first half of the period finishing their artworks.
2. As groups finish, give them a copy of their country's *History* sheet. They will use information from this sheet to evaluate their choice of artifacts.
3. If students decide that one or more of their initial choices were wrong, they may barter their artworks with other groups of curators for more appropriate display pieces. Allow them the remainder of the day to discuss their choices amongst their groups and to barter.

Day Three

1. Ask for a volunteer from each group to read their *Renaissance Country* and *History* sheets to the rest of the class.
2. Read which artifacts are needed for each section of the display.
   Italy: *Mona Lisa, Creation of Man, Pope Leo X with Two Cardinals*
   The Netherlands: *The Nativity, The Ghent Altarpiece, Altarpiece of the Last Judgment*
   France: *Francis I on Horseback, Etienne Chevalier and St. Stephen, King Francois I*
   Germany: *The Large Turf, The Knight and the Devil, Isenheim Altarpiece*
   As you call out the artifacts, the creator(s) should place the artifact in its proper spot in the museum (even if the wrong group made it).
3. Refer to the *Habits of Mind Discussion* for closure.
4. If time permits, have students complete the *Renaissance Art Quiz*.

Things to Consider

1. Students will need to buy into the idea of sifting through artifacts to create a museum; you may want to invite other classes to tour the finished museum or set up a student-guided tour of the museum for parents.
2. Read the directions carefully in order to have a clear picture of which activity sheets you need for each day, and when/how they should be distributed. A bit of time spent on preparations and organization will make the activity itself much easier.
3. On the second day, students may finish creating their artifacts at different times; encourage early finishers to add more detail or decoration before giving them history activity sheets.
4. Unlike many activities in this book, this activity is not time dependent. Encourage students to do their best work, not necessarily their fastest. If a project is substandard, ask students to continue working on it. This is especially important if inviting other classes or parents to tour the museum.
5. As the artwork task sheets are reusable, you might consider laminating them for repeated use.
6. If you ask students not to write on the sheets (especially the artwork sheets), you can reuse them in the future.

Renaissance and Reformation   *Lesson Plans*

Renaissance and Reformation (cont.)

Read-Aloud Directions

The *[insert your school's name]* Renaissance Museum just received a shipment of artworks from our acquisitions expert in Europe. Unfortunately, she didn't label the boxes! We have 12 priceless artworks, but before we can put them on display, we have to figure out which country they belong to. It would be pretty embarrassing, for example, if a museum of American artifacts put a television in the Civil War exhibit, or gave George Washington a cell phone.

Our acquisitions expert did, however, send us information about the countries of France, Germany, Italy, and the Netherlands during the Renaissance. Using this information, we will need to match artworks to countries. Some of our guesses might be wrong; we'll just have to do the best we can. Our expert said that if she found any more information, she'd send it right away.

We will be working in four groups of curators. Each group will be responsible for choosing three artworks to go in their country's museum display. When you gather with your group, your first task will be to fill out the *Renaissance Country* sheet individually. You will then use the *Artworks Master Sheet* to select your artifacts as a group. When groups are finished choosing artworks on their sheets, we will take turns picking artworks so that no two groups choose the same thing.

Once groups have artworks and have used the *Curator Tasks* sheets to decide who is working on what, you will get a sheet that describes each of the paintings you chose. If you find that once you see your paintings, you don't think they are from your country, you can trade them with other groups. Follow the directions on the sheet to create your own work of Renaissance art.

Answer Key

Renaissance Art Quiz (pages 173–174)

1. Italy
2. Germany
3. The Netherlands
4. France

5. B—Humanism
6. C—Reformation
7. A—Italy
8. D—Florence
9. B—Medici
10. Answers will vary but students should notice the detail and the realism, and should include at least five specific details.

Renaissance and Reformation *Reproducibles*

Renaissance Country: Italy

Names: _____   Date: _____

Italy is the home of the Renaissance, where artists in the city of Florence rediscovered the techniques and ideals of Roman and Greek masters. Like the Greeks and Romans, the Florentine artists of the 1400s and 1500s tried to recreate the perfection of the human form and strove to create a feeling of balance in their art. While the church was still the most powerful influence on art, rich families, such as the Medici, also commissioned paintings, which were mostly portraits.

Directions: Read the list of artworks below, and circle the five that you think were created by Renaissance Italy. You don't have all the information you need to make perfect choices, so make your best guess based on the little information given above.

Isenheim Altarpiece: This highly detailed altar panel uses thick color and feels as if it could as easily be a scene from a medieval fairytale as a story from Christianity.

The Creation of Man: This famous painting from the Sistine Chapel shows God reaching out to touch the finger of Adam.

Francis I on Horseback: This court portrait shows Francis I wearing ornamental armor and riding a highly decorated horse. The emphasis is on color and beautiful patterns.

Etienne Chevalier and Saint Stephen: This painting shows the artist's patron piously standing next to a saint.

The Ghent Altarpiece: This altarpiece is by the first artist to fully exploit the new technique of oil painting, which he uses to show minute detail and beautiful lighting.

King Francois I: This painting shows the beauty of the human form, in a way that focuses on sensuality as opposed to the mathematical perfection of the first Renaissance works. The school that created this painting started to pull away from the stylistic constraints of the church.

Renaissance Country: Italy *(cont.)*

Altarpiece of the Last Judgment: Included on an altar pane, this painting shows a white-skinned angel weighing humans on a scale.

Pope Leo X with Two Cardinals: Although simple in comparison with some of the other artworks on this list, this painting from 1518 shows the uneasy times that accompanied Luther's questioning of the Catholic Church.

Mona Lisa: Probably the world's most famous painting, the Mona Lisa has mystified generations of scholars with her perfectly proportioned face and enigmatic smile.

The Knight and the Devil: This detailed copperplate engraving incorporates themes from fantasy and mythology.

The Nativity: Many Renaissance artists painted the Nativity. This one uses realism, miniature, and Christian symbolism to pack much meaning into a small space.

The Large Turf: One of the few nonreligious and nonportrait works of the Renaissance, *The Large Turf* shows grass and flowers in amazing detail.

Renaissance and Reformation   *Reproducibles*

Renaissance Country: Germany

Names: _____ Date: _____

German art during the Renaissance was largely based on Gothic International Style, which included precise observation of the natural world, an attention to detail, a mix of Christian ideas with mythology and legend, and sometimes depictions of agonized human forms.

Directions: Read the list of artworks below, and circle the five that you think were created by Renaissance Germany. You don't have all the information you need to make perfect choices, so make your best guess based on the little information given above.

    Isenheim Altarpiece: This highly detailed altar panel uses thick color and feels as if it could as easily be a scene from a medieval fairytale as a story from Christianity.

    The Creation of Man: This famous painting from the Sistine Chapel shows God reaching out to touch the finger of Adam.

    Francis I on Horseback: This court portrait shows Francis I wearing ornamental armor and riding a highly decorated horse. The emphasis is on color and beautiful patterns.

    Etienne Chevalier and Saint Stephen: This painting shows the artist's patron piously standing next to a saint.

    The Ghent Altarpiece: This altarpiece is by the first artist to fully exploit the new technique of oil painting, which he uses to show minute detail and beautiful lighting.

    King Francois I: This painting shows the beauty of the human form, in a way that focuses on sensuality as opposed to the mathematical perfection of the first Renaissance works. The school that created this painting started to pull away from the stylistic constraints of the church.

Renaissance Country: Germany (cont.)

Altarpiece of the Last Judgment: Included on an altar pane, this painting shows a white-skinned angel weighing humans on a scale.

Pope Leo X with Two Cardinals: Although simple in comparison with some of the other artworks on this list, this painting from 1518 shows the uneasy times that accompanied Luther's questioning of the Catholic Church.

Mona Lisa: Probably the world's most famous painting, the Mona Lisa has mystified generations of scholars with her perfectly proportioned face and enigmatic smile.

The Knight and the Devil: This detailed copperplate engraving incorporates themes from fantasy and mythology.

The Nativity: Many Renaissance artists painted the Nativity. This one uses realism, miniature, and Christian symbolism to pack much meaning into a small space.

The Large Turf: One of the few nonreligious and nonportrait works of the Renaissance, *The Large Turf* shows grass and flowers in amazing detail.

Renaissance and Reformation — *Reproducibles*

Renaissance Country: France

Names: _____   Date: _____

Renaissance France was a place of kings and courts, of queens and elaborate costumes. French court painters including those at the School of Fontainebleau documented richness and the beauty of the human form.

Directions: Read the list of artworks below, and circle the five that you think were created by Renaissance France. You don't have all the information you need to make perfect choices, so make your best guess based on the little information given above.

Isenheim Altarpiece: This highly detailed altar panel uses thick color and feels as if it could as easily be a scene from a medieval fairytale as a story from Christianity.

The Creation of Man: This famous painting from the Sistine Chapel shows God reaching out to touch the finger of Adam.

Francis I on Horseback: This court portrait shows Francis I wearing ornamental armor and riding a highly decorated horse. The emphasis is on color and beautiful patterns.

Etienne Chevalier and Saint Stephen: This painting shows the artist's patron piously standing next to a saint.

The Ghent Altarpiece: This altarpiece is by the first artist to fully exploit the new technique of oil painting, which he uses to show minute detail and beautiful lighting.

King Francois I: This painting shows the beauty of the human form, in a way that focuses on sensuality as opposed to the mathematical perfection of the first Renaissance works. The school that created this painting started to pull away from the stylistic constraints of the church.

Renaissance Country: France *(cont.)*

Altarpiece of the Last Judgment: Included on an altar pane, this painting shows a white-skinned angel weighing humans on a scale.

Pope Leo X with Two Cardinals: Although simple in comparison with some of the other artworks on this list, this painting from 1518 shows the uneasy times that accompanied Luther's questioning of the Catholic Church.

Mona Lisa: Probably the world's most famous painting, the Mona Lisa has mystified generations of scholars with her perfectly proportioned face and enigmatic smile.

The Knight and the Devil: This detailed copperplate engraving incorporates themes from fantasy and mythology.

The Nativity: Many Renaissance artists painted the Nativity. This one uses realism, miniature, and Christian symbolism to pack much meaning into a small space.

The Large Turf: One of the few nonreligious and nonportrait works of the Renaissance, *The Large Turf* shows grass and flowers in amazing detail.

Renaissance and Reformation *Reproducibles*

Renaissance Country: The Netherlands

Names: _____   Date: _____

The artists of the Renaissance Netherlands were the first to fully use the technique of oil painting, which allowed them to paint in minute detail and to use bright colors and light. The paintings of the Netherlands were rarely just portraits—many displayed fanciful scenes from the Bible and were rich in Christian symbolism, packing a lot of meaning into a little space.

Directions: Read the list of artworks below and circle the five that you think were created by the Renaissance Netherlands. You don't have all the information you need to make perfect choices, so make your best guess based on the little information given above.

Isenheim Altarpiece: This highly detailed altar panel uses thick color and feels as if it could as easily be a scene from a medieval fairytale as a story from Christianity.

The Creation of Man: This famous painting from the Sistine Chapel shows God reaching out to touch the finger of Adam.

Francis I on Horseback: This court portrait shows Francis I wearing ornamental armor and riding a highly decorated horse. The emphasis is on color and beautiful patterns.

Etienne Chevalier and Saint Stephen: This painting shows the artist's patron piously standing next to a saint.

The Ghent Altarpiece: This altarpiece is by the first artist to fully exploit the new technique of oil painting, which he uses to show minute detail and beautiful lighting.

King Francois I: This painting shows the beauty of the human form, in a way that focuses on sensuality as opposed to the mathematical perfection of the first Renaissance works. The school that created this painting started to pull away from the stylistic constraints of the church.

Renaissance Country: The Netherlands (cont.)

Altarpiece of the Last Judgment: Included on an altar pane, this painting shows a white-skinned angel weighing humans on a scale.

Pope Leo X with Two Cardinals: Although simple in comparison with some of the other artworks on this list, this painting from 1518 shows the uneasy times that accompanied Luther's questioning of the Catholic Church.

Mona Lisa: Probably the world's most famous painting, the Mona Lisa has mystified generations of scholars with her perfectly proportioned face and enigmatic smile.

The Knight and the Devil: This detailed copperplate engraving incorporates themes from fantasy and mythology.

The Nativity: Many Renaissance artists painted the Nativity. This one uses realism, miniature, and Christian symbolism to pack much meaning into a small space.

The Large Turf: One of the few nonreligious and nonportrait works of the Renaissance, *The Large Turf* shows grass and flowers in amazing detail.

Renaissance and Reformation *Reproducibles*

Artworks Master Sheet

Names: _____   Date: _____

Directions: In your group, go down the list of artworks below.

- As you say each artwork, everyone who circled it on their individual sheet should raise their hand.

- Based on the number of votes that each artifact gets from your group, rank the top seven, one being the first choice, seven being the last choice.

- Your group will be making only three artifacts overall, but because the other groups might choose some of the artifacts you would like, you need to have a couple of extras.

  Isenheim Altarpiece: This highly detailed altar panel uses thick color and feels as if it could as easily be a scene from a medieval fairytale as a story from Christianity.

  The Creation of Man: This famous painting from the Sistine Chapel shows God reaching out to touch the finger of Adam.

  Francis I on Horseback: This court portrait shows Francis I wearing ornamental armor and riding a highly decorated horse. The emphasis is on color and beautiful patterns.

  Etienne Chevalier and Saint Stephen: This painting shows the artist's patron piously standing next to a saint.

  The Ghent Altarpiece: This altarpiece is by the first artist to fully exploit the new technique of oil painting, which he uses to show minute detail and beautiful lighting.

  King Francois I: This painting shows the beauty of the human form, in a way that focuses on sensuality as opposed to the mathematical perfection of the first Renaissance works. The school that created this painting started to pull away from the stylistic constraints of the church.

Artworks Master Sheet (cont.)

Altarpiece of the Last Judgment: Included on an altar pane, this painting shows a white-skinned angel weighing humans on a scale.

Pope Leo X with Two Cardinals: Although simple in comparison with some of the other artworks on this list, this painting from 1518 shows the uneasy times that accompanied Luther's questioning of the Catholic Church.

Mona Lisa: Probably the world's most famous painting, the Mona Lisa has mystified generations of scholars with her perfectly proportioned face and enigmatic smile.

The Knight and the Devil: This detailed copperplate engraving incorporates themes from fantasy and mythology.

The Nativity: Many Renaissance artists painted the Nativity. This one uses realism, miniature, and Christian symbolism to pack much meaning into a small space.

The Large Turf: One of the few nonreligious and nonportrait works of the Renaissance, *The Large Turf* shows grass and flowers in amazing detail.

Renaissance and Reformation — *Reproducibles*

Curator Tasks

Names: _____   Date: _____

Directions: Before you can start creating each of the artworks you chose, you need to figure out which curator is doing each task. Complete this sheet, making sure that people are spread out evenly, and show the finished sheet to your teacher. Once your teacher has said it's okay, you can get to work, following the directions on your artwork sheets.

Artwork/Job	Student Names
Artwork 1	
Artwork 2	
Artwork 3	

Renaissance and Reformation

Reproducibles

Mona Lisa

Names: _____   Date: _____

This famous portrait of a wealthy woman was painted using a technique called *sfumato*, in which the lines are generally soft and the figure is heavily shaded. In sfumato, shapes gradually blend into each other, instead of being separated by heavy black lines. Notice the background—again the lines are soft.

This painting is considered *humanist* because it shows a scene from the real world as opposed to a scene from the Christian religion. Humanism places an emphasis on *this* world and the beauty within it.

Directions: Answer the following questions on your own paper.

1. What do you notice first about this painting? Where do your eyes want to focus?

2. How much is "going on" in this painting? Is it busy or is it calm?

3. What does this painting tell you about the woman named Mona Lisa?

4. What do you think are Mona Lisa's emotions?

5. Now, work with your group to create a work of art similar to the *Mona Lisa*. It doesn't have to be exactly the same, but it needs to have the same answers to the questions above. Don't forget to make this a humanist portrait using the sfumato technique!

Renaissance and Reformation   *Reproducibles*

The Creation of Man

Names: _____   Date: _____

This painting is an example of the rebirth of the Greek and Roman idea of the perfection of the human body. This scene is actually only one piece of a larger painting that illustrates many stories from the Bible.

Directions: Answer the following questions on your own paper.

1. What are the vertical lines running through the painting, and why do you think they are there?

2. Who do you think is the bearded figure on the right (the painting's title is a clue)?

3. Who do you think is the man lying down on the left?

4. Where do you think each of these people are?

5. Do you think the lines of this painting are "soft" or "hard"? Would you describe it as "crisp" or "hazy"?

6. Now, work with your group to create a work of art similar to *The Creation of Man*. It doesn't have to be exactly the same, but it needs to have the same answers to the questions above. Don't forget to use soft lines to show the perfection of the human body.

Renaissance and Reformation   Reproducibles

Pope Leo X with Two Cardinals

Names: _____   Date: _____

The artist who created this painting was best known for his beautiful Madonnas and images of perfection from the classical world of the Greeks and Romans. This departure from his standard subjects reflects the attitude of the Catholic Church at the time. Later, you will see why the Catholic Church felt this way.

Directions: Answer the following questions on your own paper.

1. Where are these people looking—toward each other, toward the viewer, or somewhere else? What do you think this is supposed to mean?

2. What do you think is the emotion of the pope?

3. What do you think is the feeling of the painting? Are these people happy?

4. Would you call this painting simple or detailed? Is there a lot going on or only a little?

5. Compare the background of this painting to others that you have seen. What do you notice?

6. Now, work with your group to create a work of art similar to *Pope Leo X with Two Cardinals*. It doesn't have to be exactly the same, but it needs to have the same answers to the questions above. Don't forget to recreate the mood and the style, including the background.

Renaissance and Reformation — *Reproducibles*

The Ghent Altarpiece

Names: _____ Date: _____

This is a painting done on a wooden screen that was opened and placed around a church altar to display the art for special occasions. It is also one of the first works to use oil paints.

Directions: Answer the following questions on your own paper.

1. What do you notice first about this painting?

2. If you looked at this painting for a while, do you think you would continue to see new things? Is it simple or detailed?

3. Does this include images from real life or from religion? How can you tell?

4. Does the background look flat or does it include patterns and detail?

5. What else do you notice about this painting?

6. Now, work with your group to create a work of art similar to *The Ghent Altarpiece*. It doesn't have to be exactly the same, but it needs to have the same answers to the questions above. First, create a multipaneled "screen" using poster paper. Don't forget to use detail!

Renaissance and Reformation   Reproducibles

The Nativity

Names: _____   Date: _____

This scene is drawn from Christian religion and uses bright reds, blues, greens, and yellows. This painting combines keen observation of nature with meaningful symbols.

Directions: Answer the following questions on your own paper.

1. What do you notice first about this painting?

2. Would you say this painting is simple or detailed? Does this include the background?

3. Is this a scene from real life or from religion?

4. Is it a portrait of one person or a scene including many people?

5. Do you think the lines in this painting are fairly sharp, or does one shape blend into the next?

6. Who do you think the people are in this painting, and what are they doing?

7. Do you notice anything else about this painting?

8. Now, work with your group to create a work of art similar to this *Nativity*. It doesn't have to be exactly the same, but it needs to have the same answers to the questions above. Don't forget to recreate the mood and the style, including the background.

Renaissance and Reformation *Reproducibles*

Altarpiece of the Last Judgment

Names: _____   Date: _____

This scene from the Christian religion shows people being weighed on a balance during the Last Judgment. The painting uses bright reds, greens, and blues and was originally part of a wooden screen that could be opened around a church altar.

Directions: Answer the following questions on your own paper.

1. What do you first notice about this painting?

2. What do you think is happening to the two people on the sides of the scale?

3. What do you think is the message of this painting?

4. Do the lines look crisp, or does one shape blend into the next?

5. Would you say this painting is detailed or simple?

6. What else do you notice about this painting?

7. Now, work with your group to create a work of art similar to the *Altarpiece of the Last Judgment*. It doesn't have to be exactly the same, but it needs to have the same answers to the questions above. Don't forget to use the same colors and to include the same amount of activity.

Renaissance and Reformation — Reproducibles

The Knight and the Devil

Names: _____   Date: _____

This is originally a copperplate engraving, meaning the scene was etched (scratched) in metal. While the subject is realistically etched, the scene is not something you would see in everyday life. This detailed etching is in black and white.

Directions: Answer the following questions on your own paper.

1. What is the devil holding in his right hand?

2. What do you think he is saying to the knight?

3. Where do you think the knight is going?

4. Does the devil look like what you would expect, or does he look more like a mythological representation?

5. What do you think is the weird figure standing behind the horse?

6. What else do you notice about this etching?

7. Now, work with your group to create a work of art similar to *The Knight and the Devil*. It doesn't have to be exactly the same, but it needs to have the same answers to the questions above. Don't forget to recreate the style to the best of your ability.

Renaissance and Reformation *Reproducibles*

The Isenheim Altarpiece

Names: _____ Date: _____

This painting was part of a wooden screen that would be opened around the altar in a Christian church. The many panels of this screen would be swung open for feast days and left closed for most of the week. The colors are heavy and thick, but not necessarily bright. As you can tell, this is a fanciful scene rather than a real-life portrait.

Directions: Answer the following questions on your own paper.

1. What in this painting makes you think the scene is from the Christian religion?

2. What in this painting makes you think the scene is from medieval mythology?

3. What do you think is the story behind this picture?

4. Would you say this painting has a lot or a little going on?

5. Is it simple or detailed?

6. What else do you notice about this painting?

7. Now, work with your group to create a work of art similar to *The Isenheim Altarpiece*. It doesn't have to be exactly the same, but it needs to have the same answers to the questions above. Don't forget to use the same level of detail and color and to choose a similar subject.

Renaissance and Reformation

Reproducibles

The Large Turf

Names: _____ Date: _____

This painting shows the shift from the medieval practice of painting flowers as they *should be* (idealized) to the Renaissance practice of painting flowers as they *are* (realized). While there are many different kinds of plants, the overall impression is of a tangled clump. This painting uses almost all shades of green, with just a couple of splashes of yellow.

Directions: Answer the following questions on your own paper.

1. What do you think is the purpose of this painting?

2. Why would the artist want to paint this scene?

3. Would you say this painting is fanciful and soft or realistic and hard-lined?

4. What do you notice about this painting? Is there one subject, or does your eye roam around, noticing many different details?

5. What else do you notice about this painting?

6. Now, work with your group to create a work of art similar to *The Large Turf*. It doesn't have to be exactly the same, but it needs to have the same answers to the questions above. Don't forget to use the same level of detail and color and to choose a similar subject.

Renaissance and Reformation — *Reproducibles*

Etienne Chevalier and Saint Stephen

Names: _____   Date: _____

In this painting, a rich patron commissioned the artist to paint his portrait with Saint Stephen. The Bible tells that Saint Stephen was the first Christian martyr—he was stoned to death for refusing to stop preaching the teachings of Jesus.

Directions: Answer the following questions on your own paper.

1. What do you think is the object on top of the book (clue: remember the story of Saint Stephen)?

2. Which person do you think is the patron and which is the saint? Why do you think this?

3. Why do you think this patron had his picture painted with the saint? What is the patron trying to say?

4. Does this painting include a great deal of detail, or are there only a few things to look at?

5. Would you say this painting is fanciful or realistic? Why?

6. Now, work with your group to create a work of art similar to *Etienne Chevalier and Saint Stephen*. It doesn't have to be exactly the same, but it needs to have the same answers to the questions above. Don't forget to use the same level of detail and color and to choose a similar subject. Make sure you include something that tells us the identity of your people.

Renaissance and Reformation — Reproducibles

Francis I on Horseback

Names: _____ Date: _____

The artist used rich blues, reds, and gold to paint this portrait of King Francis I.

Directions: Answer the following questions on your own paper.

1. What do you think is the purpose of this painting?

2. What in the painting tells you this person was a king?

3. Although the king is wearing armor, do you think he is dressed for battle or dressed for show? How can you tell?

4. Is the horse dressed for battle or for show? How can you tell?

5. Does this portrait look posed, or is this a scene from everyday life? How can you tell?

6. What else do you notice about this painting?

7. Now, work with your group to create a work of art similar to *Francis I on Horseback*. It doesn't have to be exactly the same, but it needs to have the same answers to the questions above. Don't forget to use the same level of detail and color and to choose a similar subject.

Renaissance and Reformation *Reproducibles*

King Francois I

Names: _____   Date: _____

This portrait was painted around 1530. Its flowing lines and soft colors are similar to the Italian school of Renaissance paintings. We also see the attention to the human form that makes this a humanist work.

Directions: Answer the following questions on your own paper.

1. What adjectives would you use to describe this painting (examples: flowing, soft, kind)?

2. Do you think this painting is of a common person or someone from the royal family? Why?

3. Do you think this painting looks posed or natural? Why do you think this?

4. What is the focus of this painting? What is the first thing your eyes see?

5. What else do you notice about this painting?

6. Now, work with your group to create a work of art similar to *King Francois I*. It doesn't have to be exactly the same, but it needs to have the same answers to the questions above. Don't forget to use the same techniques and to use a subject similar to the one in this painting.

Renaissance and Reformation   *Reproducibles*

History: Italy

Names: _____ Date: _____

Directions: Answer the questions below, and use these clues to help you decide if the artworks you created are the correct ones for Italy. If not, you can trade with other groups for more appropriate pieces for your museum display. Italy was the home of the Renaissance for the following five reasons.

The Church—The early Renaissance was a stable time for the church in Italy. Instead of church leaders battling with each other for power, the Renaissance saw one pope in control, who was able to spend his energy building many new churches and redecorating some old ones. Some of the most important works of Renaissance art in Italy were painted directly on church walls and ceilings. Later in the Renaissance, Italian painters were able to use their skill to show the uncertainty of the Catholic Church.

Question: Which one artwork do you now think is definitely from Renaissance Italy?

_____

Question: Is there another painting that shows the uncertainty of the church that might be from later in the Renaissance?

_____

Florence—The cities of Italy no longer fought each other with swords and bows, but they did compete to be known as the leading city of Italy. For Florence, this meant outdoing its neighbors in art, architecture, and culture.

Question: How did Florence influence Renaissance art?

_____
_____

History: Italy (cont.)

Humanism—Humanism is a school of thought that valued everyday life instead of just the Christian afterlife. Due to humanism, artists were able to paint portraits of real people instead of just figures from the Bible, and they sometimes included real landscapes in their paintings. One of these portraits, by Leonardo da Vinci, shows a young Florentine woman with slight smile against a landscape background.

Question: Which one artwork do you now think is definitely from Renaissance Italy?

_____

The Medici Family—Because Florence was a republic, it was ruled by laws instead of by a king. The wealthy Medici family couldn't just become rulers; they had to find other ways to make themselves the leading family of Italy. The way the Medicis did this was to pay for art. Everybody knew that the Medicis were the reason Florence was so beautiful, and for this, everybody loved the Medicis.

Question: Are there any modern families that have given to arts and culture like the Medicis? Name them.

_____

_____

The "Door" Contest—The baptistery next to the cathedral known as the Duomo needed new bronze doors. The city of Florence had an artist competition to see who would get to make these doors. This competition was a huge deal and the winner, named Ghiberti, became famous. Before this competition, artists were just like furniture makers or architects, but after the door contest, artists became superstars just like today's sports heroes or movie stars.

Question: What do you think was the effect of fame on the arts?

_____

_____

_____

_____

Renaissance and Reformation — *Reproducibles*

History: France

Names: _____ Date: _____

Directions: Read the excerpts, answer the questions below, and use these clues to evaluate your choice of artworks. If you find that some of your initial choices are wrong, you can trade them with other groups. Try to end up with the three works of art that are from Renaissance France.

Francis I was the first Renaissance king of France. While the kings before him were concerned with Italy, they cared mostly whether or not the Italians were going to attack. Francis cared about Italy, too, but he cared much more about their ideas in art, literature, and architecture. King Francis I hired people to tour Italy in search of great works of art that could be shipped back to France. Because of this, the Renaissance in France was based on the Renaissance of Italy, and many of the French works of art look similar to Italian paintings.

Question: If *The Creation of Man* is an Italian work of art, which other work of art looks similar, and could be French (don't tell the Italian curators you know one of their artworks!)?

_____

_____

Francis I was responsible for France's first great Renaissance buildings, known as "chateaus," which were highly decorated castles. Outside the royal chateau of Fontainebleau there was a grand fountain in which the water was mixed with wine. This idea of ornamental decoration carried over into clothing, interior design, and art. The School of Fontainebleau was known for portraits of royalty in beautiful clothing.

Question: Which one painting is a portrait of someone in highly decorated clothing?

_____

Francis I was a humanist, meaning he believed in the importance of enjoying everyday life, as opposed to just being concerned with the Christian afterlife. The humanist ideas were seen in art as an emphasis on the beauty of the human form, which was sometimes painted nude or with flowing clothes that accentuated the body.

Question: How do you think humanism differs from Christianity?

_____

_____

Renaissance and Reformation   *Reproducibles*

History: Germany

Names: _____   Date: _____

Directions: Read the excerpts, answer the questions below, and use these clues to evaluate your choice of artworks. If you find that some of your initial choices are wrong, you can trade them with other groups. Try to end up with the three works of art that are from Renaissance Germany.

While Renaissance Italy and France had turned to humanism, in which painters depicted the beauty and joy of the human form, Germany held onto medieval ideas of fantasy and myth. This fantasy included mixing Christian tradition with that of fairies and folk tales.

Question: Which two paintings look like they include elements of fairy tales?

_____

_____

French and Italian painters tended to focus on one figure and painted many portraits, but German artists drew their ideas from the Bible or from nature and tended to pack much detail into a small space. Be careful—the artists from the Netherlands did this, too!

Question: Which paintings could you cross off as possibilities?

_____

_____

On October 31, 1517, a monk named Martin Luther nailed his ideas to the door of the Castle Church. This event marks the start of the Reformation, in which the Lutheran and Protestant churches broke away from Catholic tradition. The Reformation in England led to people getting rid of art in their churches, but in Germany it helped artists develop a style that was distinctly different from the Italians. If you can figure out which art is from the Italian Renaissance, you might be able to choose the German art by picking the ones that look the most different.

There are three paintings on your list that are altarpieces, meaning they were painted on the panels of wooden screens that could be folded out to display the paintings for special occasions. Only one of these altarpieces is from the German Renaissance.

Question: Compare the three altarpieces (you might need to look at other groups' artwork sheets). Based on the ideas on this sheet, which one do you think is from Renaissance Germany?

_____

©Shell Educational Publishing   171   #9357 *Hands-on History: World History Activities*

Renaissance and Reformation   *Reproducibles*

History: The Netherlands

Names: _____ Date: _____

Directions: Read the excerpts, answer the questions below, and use these clues to evaluate your choice of artworks. If you find that some of your initial choices are wrong, you can trade them with other groups. Try to end up with the three works of art that are from the Renaissance Netherlands.

Like Germany, the Netherlands was late to embrace humanism, in which Italian and French artists painted portraits that showed the beauty of the human form. Most art from the Netherlands did not show real people.

Question: Based on this information, which paintings can you cross off your list?

_____

Unlike German paintings, art from the Netherlands rarely mixed elements of folk tales such as fairies and wizards with scenes of Christianity.

Question: Based on this information, which paintings can you cross off your list?

_____

The artist Jan van Eyck was the first to successfully use the new technique of oil painting, which allowed him to paint minute detail and to highlight the effects of light. Many paintings of the Renaissance in the Netherlands included bright colors, miniaturized detail, and Christian symbolism.

Question: Which painting(s) do you think show these features?

_____

The Renaissance in the Netherlands was shortlived. On October 31, 1517 a monk named Martin Luther nailed his ideas to the door of the Castle Church in Germany. This event marks the start of the Reformation, in which the Lutheran and Protestant churches broke away from Catholic tradition. Late in the 16th century, the Reformation led people of the Netherlands to get rid of most of the art in churches because they thought it led people to worship the art and not God. The Protestant and Lutheran faiths that developed during the Reformation taught that people didn't need priests in order to find God and translated the Bible from Latin so that common people could read it for themselves.

Question: How was the Reformation good for people?

_____

Question: How was the Reformation bad for art?

_____

Renaissance and Reformation Reproducibles

Renaissance Art Quiz

Name: _____ Date: _____

Directions: Four paintings are described below. Draw a line connecting them with the correct country.

1. A scene from the Bible showing idealized nude angels that look like they are from Greek or Roman times, painted using the sfumato technique to make soft, blended lines.	France
2. A highly detailed copperplate etching that blends Christianity with medieval folklore, such as fairies.	Germany
3. An oil painting that uses bright blues, yellows, greens, and reds to show a miniaturized fantasy scene from the Bible, incorporating Christian symbolism.	The Netherlands
4. A highly decorated portrait of a rich, beautiful queen that shows the beauty of the human body.	Italy

Directions: Circle the best answer to the following questions

5. The idea that the everyday world of this life was to be enjoyed, as opposed to just worrying about the Christian afterlife was called

    A. hedonism.   C. reformation.
    B. humanism.   D. classicism.

6. The monk Martin Luther nailed his ideas to the Castle Church in Germany, starting the

    A. Civil War.   C. Reformation
    B. 100-Years War   D. Catholic Church.

Renaissance and Reformation — *Reproducibles*

Renaissance Art Quiz (cont.)

Name: _____ Date: _____

7. Which country was the home of the Renaissance?

    A. Italy
    B. France
    C. Germany
    D. The Netherlands

8. In which city did the Renaissance start?

    A. Paris
    B. Frankfurt
    C. Ghent
    D. Florence

9. What was the name of the most important family of Renaissance art patrons?

    A. Gates
    B. Medici
    C. Michelangelo
    D. Mellon

10. On the back of this sheet, describe the painting below in your own words, including at least five details. What is going on and what techniques are used? Be specific!

#9357 *Hands-on History: World History Activities*   174   ©*Shell Educational Publishing*

Habits of Mind Discussion

- How is the art of Renaissance Germany, France, Italy, and the Netherlands different?

- Which countries are the most similar? Why?

- How did the Reformation affect Renaissance art?

- What made Italy the center of the Renaissance?

- History happened in the past. Does this mean it can't change?

- Did every painting fit its country's style? Do you think that sometimes individuals break from the style of their times?

A Century of Turmoil: 1940–2001 Lesson Plans

A Century of Turmoil: 1940–2001

Overview

In this activity, students will explore online oral histories that describe some of the 20th century's most difficult events, focusing on those that affected the United States. Specifically, students will compare the attitudes surrounding World War II, the Holocaust, and Pearl Harbor with the testimonies of September 11, 2001, survivors.

Please be aware that this can be an emotionally difficult activity, and you will want to assign mature students to the 9/11 and Holocaust histories.

The destruction at Pearl Harbor
Source: Corbis

Depending on your technology resources, you can ask students to complete the activity individually or in small groups or perform the research as a teacher-guided lesson by attaching a projector to one computer. Alternately (with older classes), you can have students complete the research portion of the activity as homework. In an optional extension, students may gather their own oral histories and present them to the class.

Objectives

- Students will describe the ways nations and organizations respond to forces of unity and diversity affecting order and security. (NCSS)
- Students will appreciate how technology offers access to otherwise obscure information.

Materials

- copies of reproducibles (pages 180–190) as described on page 177
- computers with Internet access
- headphones (optional)
- poster paper
- colored pens/pencils

A Century of Turmoil: 1940–2001 Lesson Plans

A Century of Turmoil: 1940–2001 *(cont.)*

Preparation

Total preparation time should be about 5 minutes.

1. Copy the *Oral History Search* sheets (pages 180–185), such that each student can have at least one. You may ask students to complete additional search sheets based on the amount of time you choose to spend with this activity (and based on how quickly students complete their first sheets).

2. Make a classroom set of the *Century of Turmoil Reflective Writing* (page 189), the *Oral History Directions* (page 186), the *Oral History Planning* sheet (page 187), and the *Oral History Questions* sheet (page 188).

3. Reserve or otherwise gather needed technology. For many of the oral history sites listed, you will need the application RealPlayer installed, which can be downloaded for free at **http://www.real.com**. You may want to test your technology by visiting one of the listed oral history sites before completing the activity with students.

4. If you feel your class may have difficulty with the material, send home permission slips before beginning the activity.

Directions

1. After reading the *Read-Aloud Directions* (page 178), distribute *Oral History Search* sheets and start the activity. Make sure that students visit only the sites included on their sheets (or they are likely to waste considerable time searching).

2. Once students have finished their search sheets, have them gather with the people who completed the same sheets to create a presentation of the information they found. Each group should make a poster that combines the information from their individual *Oral History Search* sheets. Especially encourage students to include oral history quotes on their posters and, if possible, to illustrate the speakers.

3. After finishing presentations, have students complete the *Century of Turmoil Reflective Writing* assignment and then close with the *Habits of Mind Discussion* (page 190).

Optional Extension:

If technology resources permit, have students include in their presentations audio from the oral histories they found. A good way to do this is to have students import audio into a PowerPoint presentation or simply to download audio clips to the computer desktop. When groups present, it is useful to connect the computer to speakers or to a projector with built-in speakers.

Optional Extension:

After exploring online oral history resources, ask students to complete a firsthand interview of a parent, grandparent, or older acquaintance using the included *Oral History Directions* (page 186), *Oral History Planning* sheet (page 187), and the *Oral History Questions* sheet (page 188). Have students present their oral histories to the class.

A Century of Turmoil: 1940–2001 *(cont.)*

Things to Consider

1. If you have limited computer resources, you can ask students to work with partners or in small groups. Likewise, if certain students are not yet confident readers/typists, you can support them by grouping them with able classmates.
2. Unlike many of the activities in this book, this is not a competition. You may need to remind students that you will be collecting their individual search sheets and giving a quiz at the end of the activity.
3. You will probably want to visit all of the sites before your student do so that you are familiar with them and can answer student questions as needed.

Read-Aloud Directions

History is not just something we read about in books—it's something that real people lived. In fact, we are living history right now. Some history, like your baseball team winning the World Series, is exciting and fun; other history, like the Holocaust during World War II, is difficult. The twentieth century was filled with both kinds of history—the good and the bad. And because the twentieth century was also a time of great technological change, we can now step outside the history books to explore it.

Today, we're going to use the Internet to look at what real people have to say about the history they lived. Instead of reading what a historian has written, we will hear accounts from people who were actually there. These accounts are called "oral histories." Some of these oral histories will be difficult—history can be emotional! It's okay to be disturbed by some of these accounts, and it's also okay to think that some of the accounts are a bit funny, even if they describe horrible events. Keep in mind that because these are real people, they are free to describe events however they choose.

Each of you will get an *Oral History Search* sheet, which will guide you in exploring a certain event. Once you have all completed your sheets, you will get together with the other students who completed the same sheet and will prepare a presentation for the class. Unlike some of the other activities we have done, there is no competition in this one. Also, while you will be looking at interesting information, not all of it is fun. Please visit only the website(s) listed on your sheet.

[Distribute Oral History Search *sheets, and begin the activity.]*

A Century of Turmoil: 1940–2001 (cont.)

Answer Key

Oral History Search

World War II (page 180)
1. Great Depression
2. To get a job
3. From "Eyes and Ears of the World," the newsreel shown during movies
4. He considers them elite troops, "the best of the best."
5. Mail ships were frequently torpedoed.
6. Geronimo!
7. They gathered by church steeples.
8. He was hit with a grenade and left for dead and was then further injured by a metal fragment.
9. Answers will vary. Students should list two quotes from the oral history.

The Holocaust (page 181)
1. He arranged for her to be hidden.
2. She would have been shot instantly.
3. Belgium
4. Answers will vary.
5. Eva Galler
6. Because the train was taking everybody aboard to their deaths.
7. Parents and young children
8. Because the star was how Nazis recognized Jews.
9. She pretended she was Catholic.
10. Answers will vary.

September 11, 2001 (#1) (page 182)
1. A fifth-grade student living in New York City
2. The school brought students to the auditorium where they were told the news and then continued the day with as much normalcy as possible.
3. Answers will vary but can include feeling scared, disbelieving, and/or confused as to the extent of the catastrophe.

September 11, 2001 (#1) (cont.)
4. She "thinks it's getting better and better, but it's still kind of scary."
5. Answers will vary.

September 11, 2001 (#2) (page 183)
1. A 37-year-old NYPD officer
2. She responded to "unknown conditions at the WTC" as broadcast over her radio.
3. Answers will vary but can include falling debris, huge hunks of metal, and/or a plane sticking out of the building.
4. She helped to evacuate people from inside the towers.
5. She was thrown from the safety of the building and blinded by thick smoke. She finally found a person, named Richie, who pulled her back to safety.
6. Her pocketbook—the woman was in shock.
7. Answers will vary.

Reaction to Pearl Harbor (pages 184–185)
1. A recent immigrant with a thick accent
2. He felt very positive about Roosevelt's speech and thought that after the war the world would "live in peace forever."
3. He hopes it will be short and quick.
4. He is extremely positive concerning the president and says he "thanks God that we have a great man above us who is our president."
5. Answers will vary.
6. He is behind the decision 100 percent.
7. Germany
8. He thinks Germany is in the wrong.
9. The university student sees less of a clear-cut answer than the rest of the interviewees.
10. Answers will vary.

A Century of Turmoil: 1940–2001 *Reproducibles*

Oral History Search: World War II

Name: _____   Date: _____

Go to: **http://oralhistory.minds.tv**
Click "Veteran Stories"
Click "World War II"
Click "Donald Burgett–WWII Army Paratroopers Veteran"
Follow the screen directions to listen to the audio. *Get your teacher's help to register, if necessary.*

1. What was going on in the country while Mr. Burgett was growing up?
   _____

2. Before World War II, what was his dream?
   _____

3. How did he hear news about the war?
   _____

4. What is Mr. Burgett's opinion of the Army paratroopers?
   _____

5. Skip to minute 12:40. When Mr. Burgett was in England, why did only some of the mail arrive?
   _____

6. Skip to minute 17:50. What was the famous battle cry of the paratroopers?
   _____

7. Skip to minute 23:40. How did troops who had been split up know where to meet each other?
   _____

8. Skip to minute 29:10. How was Mr. Burgett wounded?
   _____

9. List at least two quotes from the interview that you find interesting.
   _____
   _____

A Century of Turmoil: 1940–2001   Reproducibles

Oral History Search: The Holocaust

Name: _____ Date: _____

Go to: **http://www.holocaustsurvivors.org**
Click on "Audio Gallery"
Click on "Simply because we were Jews"
Follow the screen directions to listen to the audio.

1. How did Ms. Burk's father help her survive the Holocaust?
   _____

2. What would have happened to the woman who hid Ms. Burk had the woman been caught?
   _____

3. In which country did Ms. Burk spend the war?
   _____

4. List a quote from "Simply Because We Were Jews" that you find interesting.
   _____

Go to: **http://www.holocaustsurvivors.org**
Click on "Audio Gallery"
Click on "Escaping the Death Camp Train"
Follow the screen directions to listen to the audio.

5. What is the name of the person being interviewed?
   _____

6. Why did the people try to escape from the train?
   _____

7. Who stayed on the train?
   _____

8. Why did Ms. Galler refuse to wear a star from that point on?
   _____

9. How did Ms. Galler survive the remainder of the war?
   _____

10. Write a quote from "Escaping the Death Camp Train" that you find interesting.
    _____

A Century of Turmoil: 1940–2001   *Reproducibles*

Oral History Search: September 11, 2001 (#1)

Name: _____ Date: _____

Go to: **http://memory.loc.gov**
Click on "Browse"
Click on "Sound Recordings" (on the right)
Click on "September 11, 2001, and Public Reactions"
Click on "Audio"
Click on "Interview with Amanda Mummery" (in alphabetical order).
Follow the screen directions to listen to the audio.

1. Who is Amanda Mummery?
   _____

2. Describe how her school handled the September 11 attacks.
   _____

3. What did Amanda feel at school that day?
   _____

4. How does she feel at the time of the interview?
   _____

5. List three quotes from the interview that you find interesting.
   _____
   _____
   _____
   _____
   _____
   _____
   _____

A Century of Turmoil: 1940–2001 *Reproducibles*

Oral History Search: September 11, 2001 (#2)

Name: _____ Date: _____

Go to: **http://memory.loc.gov**
Click on "Browse"
Click on "Sound Recordings" (on the right)
Click on "September 11, 2001, and Public Reactions"
Click on "Audio"
Click on "Interview with Carol Paukner" (in alphabetical order)
Follow screen directions to listen to the audio.

1. Who is Carol Paukner?
   _____

2. How did she hear about the September 11 attacks?
   _____

3. What did she see after she ran to the World Trade Center?
   _____

4. What did she do once she got to the World Trade Center?
   _____

5. What happened to her when the second plane hit?
   _____

6. Skip to minute 17:10. What was the woman standing in the middle of the street looking for?
   _____

7. List at least three quotes from this oral history that you find interesting.
   _____
   _____
   _____

A Century of Turmoil: 1940–2001 Reproducibles

Oral History Search: Reaction to Pearl Harbor

Name: _____ Date: _____

Go to: **http://memory.loc.gov**
Click on "Browse"
Click on "Sound Recordings"
Click on "Pearl Harbor and Public Reactions"
Click on "List of Recordings"
Click on the fourth item in the list: "AFS6362-6364"
Click on "Man-on-the-Street" disc #3
Click to play the audio

Tape #3: Side A

1. Describe the first person recorded.

   _____

2. What is this person's attitude about President Roosevelt's speech?

   _____

3. What does the second person, who is a telephone operator and veteran of World War I, hope for this war?

   _____

4. How does the fourth person, who is a substitute postal carrier, feel about President Roosevelt?

   _____

5. List at least two quotes from this side of the tape that you find interesting.

   _____

   _____

   _____

   _____

A Century of Turmoil: 1940–2001 Reproducibles

Oral History Search: Reaction to Pearl Harbor *(cont.)*

Tape #3: Side B

6. What does the first person, who is a clerical worker, think about the decision to go to war?

   _____
   _____
   _____

7. From where did the second person interviewed emigrate?

   _____

8. What is this person's attitude about his home country?

   _____
   _____
   _____
   _____

9. What does the university student think about the war?

   _____
   _____
   _____
   _____

10. List one quote from this side of the tape that you find interesting.

    _____
    _____
    _____

A Century of Turmoil: 1940–2001   *Reproducibles*

Oral History Directions

Name: _____ Date: _____

Directions: Use the directions below to collect an oral history of someone you know.

1. **Contact the person you will interview.**

   When you talk to the person you want to interview, make sure you tell him or her the purpose of the interview and explain how it will be used. Also, let the person know the types of questions you will be asking.

2. **Prepare for the interview.**

   List three things you already know about this person. List the one thing you are most curious to learn from this person. List three questions you will ask this person.

3. **Schedule a time and place.**

   Make sure you pick a time and place where there will be little interruption.

4. **Choose your equipment.**

   Will you tape record or videotape the interview? Gather any equipment you need, and make sure you know how to use it.

5. **Start your interview with easy questions.**

   Make sure you write down the interviewee's name, approximate age, and where the interview is taking place. Start by gathering background information about your subject, such as where he or she grew up, what job he or she does, etc.

6. **Ask open-ended questions.**

   Don't ask questions that can be answered with a simple yes or no.

7. **Try to make your questions short and the answers long.**

   The more the interviewee talks, the better oral history you will collect.

A Century of Turmoil: 1940–2001 Reproducibles

Oral History Planning

Name: _____ Date: _____

Directions: Complete this sheet with all the information about the person you are going to interview and how you are going to conduct the interview.

Name of subject

_____

Contact details

_____

_____

_____

Time and place of interview

_____

_____

Preparation for the interview

_____

_____

_____

Equipment needed for the interview

_____

_____

_____

Other considerations

_____

_____

A Century of Turmoil: 1940–2001 *Reproducibles*

Oral History Questions

Name: _____ Date: _____

Directions: Use the space below to brainstorm the topics and questions you would like to ask the person you are interviewing. On the lines at the bottom of the sheet, write the final questions you will ask. Make sure you finish by thanking the person for his or her time.

_____

_____

_____

_____

_____

_____

_____

_____

A Century of Turmoil: 1940–2001   *Reproducibles*

Oral History Planning

Name: _____ Date: _____

Directions: Complete this sheet with all the information about the person you are going to interview and how you are going to conduct the interview.

Name of subject

_____

Contact details

_____
_____
_____

Time and place of interview

_____
_____

Preparation for the interview

_____
_____
_____

Equipment needed for the interview

_____
_____
_____

Other considerations

_____
_____

A Century of Turmoil: 1940–2001   *Reproducibles*

Oral History Questions

Name: _____ Date: _____

Directions: Use the space below to brainstorm the topics and questions you would like to ask the person you are interviewing. On the lines at the bottom of the sheet, write the final questions you will ask. Make sure you finish by thanking the person for his or her time.

A Century of Turmoil: 1940–2001   *Reproducibles*

A Century of Turmoil Reflective Writing

Name: _____ Date: _____

1. Describe how the person you listened to felt about the event he or she experienced.

   _____
   _____
   _____
   _____

2. List three details this person talked about that you think few other people would know.

   _____
   _____
   _____

3. How did the interview you listened to make you feel?

   _____
   _____
   _____

4. Do you think that technology has done good or bad things for the world as a whole? Give examples to support your opinion.

   _____
   _____
   _____
   _____

5. What are the advantages and disadvantages of oral history compared to written history?

   _____
   _____
   _____
   _____
   _____
   _____

Habits of Mind Discussion

- What are the advantages and disadvantages of oral history compared to written history?

- Which oral account that we listened to did you find most powerful? Why?

- What are the differences in attitudes between the people interviewed about WWII and the people interviewed about September 11, 2001?

- How do you think the county's attitude has changed between WWII and now?

- If you could remove one of these events from history, which would you choose and why?

- Which of these events do you think has had the most powerful impact on the way we live our lives?

World History

Scoring Guides

Directions: Teachers can use this scoring guide and the one on the following page to assess independent student work.

Name		Date		
5 Points Student was productive, respectful, and collaborated well with others.	**4 Points** Student was productive and respectful.	**3 Points** Student completed work when reminded.	**2 Points** Student did not work well.	**1 Point** Student was interfering with others' work.

Teacher Comments:

Parent Signature:

©Shell Educational Publishing

World History

Scoring Guides *(cont.)*

Name _____ Date _____

	Exceptional	Strong	Capable	Developing	Beginning	Emergent
	Student shows interest and enthusiasm; understands concepts and demonstrates learning; participates very well independently and in a group; produces high quality work on assignments; extends self beyond requirements; and uses a variety of resources.	Student shows interest and enthusiasm; demonstrates understanding of concepts; participates very well independently and in a group; produces high quality work on assignments; sometimes extends self beyond requirements; and sometimes uses additional resources.	Student shows interest; understands concepts; participates independently and in a group; and meets basic requirements.	Student shows interest occasionally; understands most concepts; participates infrequently; and sometimes meets basic requirements on assignments.	Student interest is not evident; understands some concepts; limited participation; and needs support to produce assignments.	Student shows little interest; understanding of concepts is limited; exerts minimal participation; and struggles to produce assignments.
	6 Points	**5 Points**	**4 Points**	**3 Points**	**2 Points**	**1 Point**

Description of Student Assignment

_____
_____
_____

Teacher Comments:

Parent Signature: